HOT ROD

AN AMERICAN ORIGINAL

PETER VINCENT

 MBI Publishing Company

DEDICATION

This book is dedicated to Kim and Nathan, for their support, help, assistance and understanding.

First published in 2001 by MBI Publishing Company, Galtier Plaza, Suite 200, 380 Jackson Street, St. Paul, MN 55101-3885, USA.

© Peter Vincent, 2001

MBI Publishing Company books are also available at discounts in bulk quantity for industrial or sales-promotional use. For details write to Special Sales Manager at Motorbooks International Wholesalers & Distributors, Galtier Plaza, Suite 200, 380 Jackson Street, St. Paul, MN 55101-3885, USA.

Library of Congress Cataloging-in-Publication Data

Vincent, Peter, 1945-
  Hot rod: an American original/Peter Vincent.
    p. cm.
  Includes index.
  ISBN 0-7603-0956-6 (hc. : alk. paper)
  1. Hot rods—United States. I. Title.

TL236.3 .V56 2001
629.228'6'0973–dc21   2001034527

On the front cover: Gene McKinney owned this chopped 1932 Ford 5-window highboy coupe when it was photographed at the 50th Bonneville Anniversary event in 1998. The other historical part of the photograph is the background, which is the old "Enola Gay" hanger at the Wendover Airport, used during WWII for training the flight crew.

On the frontispiece: Harold and Martha Aschenbrenner's 1932 Ford Hiboy roadster. Harold is a long time hot rodder and wanted to build a hemi powered 1932 Hiboy. He actually had a Chevy big block in the frame, but he ran into the right Hemi valve covers at a yard sale and changed it over to the 1956 354-cid Chrysler engine, backed by a Chrysler 4-speed tranny, and a Ford 9-inch rear. The chopped top, American five-spoke wheels, and rolled and pleated dark red Masine Vinyl help complete the look.

On the endpapers: Jerry Helwig's 1940 Ford Coupe. Most of the custom work on the Coupe was done in the 1950s by the Boyd Brothers. The body modifications include a chop top, body sectioning with the fenders molded to the body, 1937 DeSoto bumpers, and 1941 Studebaker taillights. For Bonneville, Jerry was running a 270-cid early flathead, ported and relieved, Offenhauser heads, Arias pistons, a John DeLong ground cam, Belond headers, and a Kinsler fuel injection system. The engine horsepower passed through a Doug Nash 5-speed transmission before reaching the Halibrand V-8 quickchange rear end.

On the title page: Joe Davis picked up this 1926 Model T Touring as a project in 1992. Some of the body modifications on it include rolled and louvered rocker panels, chin spoiler, 3-piece aluminum hood with side louvers, and a 6-inch chopped and laid back windshield. The front seat was moved back four inches and down two inches for comfort. The Model A chassis was shortered and narrowed, and the 1932 rear frame horns protrude through the rear of the tub with a spreader bar and 1934 taillights mounted on 1932 arms. The 1935 Ford wire wheel centers were welded to VW rims in front, and 7-inch Fords in back for the big and little wide white tire combination.

On the back cover-top: "Flathead Jack" Schafer's 1949 Merc. This traditional custom looks as good without the louvered hood in place because you can see the 276-inch flathead that gets this machine down the road. The top was cut 5 inches in the front and 4 1/2 in the rear with the rear window laid down rather than cut, which gives more visibility and blends in the lines of the trunk. The suspension was reworked by Greg Westbury, and the flames were painted by Art Himsel.

On the back cover-bottom: Dennis and Debbie Kyle's 1932 roadster. This roadster body and frame came from Tom Senter, a legendary hot rodder. The stance is a key part to the look and the 5 1/2-inch dropped axle, held in place with traditional hairpins, helps, as does the big and little tire combination. The Halibrand V-8 quickchange rear end is supported via ladder bars and a transverse buggy spring setup. The pinstriping was done by Dennis Rickliff. The engine is a 283-ci Chevy small-block and the transmission is a Muncie four-speed.

Back page: A rear view of Jim "Jake" Jacobs' well-known 1934 Coupe is a very fitting end to the book. The vehicle was photographed at the first Muroc Reunion in the mid-1990s during a very dusty weekend.

Edited by: Steve Hendrickson
Designed by: Katie Sonmor

Printed in Hong Kong

CONTENTS

ACKNOWLEDGMENTS

I would like to express a formal thank you to the following people for their help, which enabled me to write and publish this book: Dain Gingerelli, for introducing me to Keith Mathiowetz, who was the MBI editor in charge of getting this effort off and running. Steve Hendrickson, an MBI editor, for patience and guidance on the editing and final important lap of the project. A very special thanks goes out to all those whose literary contributions added to a "photographer's" text: Vern Tardel, for taking the time for the interview, especially so late at night and after such a long day out on the salt; Dick Page, for your valuable knowledge, experience, and comments in the custom chapter; Mike Bishop, for your comments on traditional 1940s and 1950s hot rods; Bill Vinther, for your comments on late 1950s/early 1960s hot rods; Jay Fitzhugh, for your comments on the Bonneville experience; Philip Linhares, for the observations and kind words in the introduction; and Pat Ganahl, for the foreword to the book. I am honored that you all thought it worthwhile and took the time to share your thoughts and valued experience.

Thanks also to the following people: Nathan Vincent, for assisting in many of the photo shoots; Curt Giovanine, for use and inclusion of images from Bob Giovanine's scrapbook; Charlie Markley, for supplying historical photographs; Joaquin Arnett, for historical information and great stories; Ron Jolliffe, for all the times we talked about this project, the trips to Muroc, and everywhere else, including the ride; Greg and JoAnn Carlson, with BNI and the SCTA, for the access and friendship; Cotton Werksman, for spending time on the phone explaining the early history of the National Street Rod Association; and to Paul and Marcia Wingfield, for the last-minute light table, which aided immensely in the final visual selection.

Most of all though, this could not have happened without all the hot rodders, racers, street rodders, and customizers out there whom I have come to know through the years. Thanks to all of you who allowed me the time to photograph your cars, especially those who waited with me for that late evening light and had the patience for the whole photographic process. And last of all, the "Bonehead Boys"—thanks to all of you for the good times and Southern California hospitality.

Some people call our cars rolling sculpture. Uh uh. Hot rods are not art. Hot rods are not built to sit still and have their pictures taken. Hot rods are not built to pose in galleries. Hot rods are built to burn rubber. In fact, a photograph cannot begin to capture the essence of a hot rod. Even in three dimensions, a hot rod at rest is a mere fraction of itself. Until you hear the WAP! of the engine; until you feel the vibrations; until you smell the vapors of gasoline/oil/rubber, you have no idea what a hot rod is. Even the smooth and sensuous customs, which come much closer to some form of sculpture, cannot be comprehended while they're sitting still. Until you sink into the sumptuous tuck-and-roll, squint through that slit windshield, and cruise slowly through the crowded drive-in while the dual exhausts burble, you have no idea what a custom car is.

Now imagine strapping yourself into the roll cage of a needle-nosed streamliner, hearing the supercharged/fuel-injected/nitro-fueled hemi engine bark to life, and then hurtle at more than 200, 300, or 400 miles an hour across the vast Bonneville salt flats. Get my drift?

Some people think that photographing hot rods or custom cars is art. Uh uh. Even if they were art objects, taking pictures of them doesn't constitute art. Photos of Rodin's *The Thinker* or Van Gogh's *Still Life with Sunflowers* are photos of a bronze sculpture and a painting, that's all. Admittedly, a photo of a hot rod is much more visually interesting than a picture of a stock '75 Ford Granada or a Checker taxi cab. But it isn't art.

Now, there *is* an art to building a hot rod or a custom car. Each of these cars is handcrafted, either by the owner or some professional builder directed by the owner, to make a personal statement. It's like the clothes you choose to wear in the morning, or the way you comb your hair. In the case of a race car, often function influences form. But you can build a rod or custom any way you want. There are no written rules. Yet, some get it right, many others get it wrong, and the rest either come close or just play it safe. It takes a real hot rodder to tell the difference.

Some people think that anyone who can operate a camera competently is a photographer. Uh uh. There are plenty of books and magazines full of photographs of hot rods, customs, and race cars. Some are better than others. I've done a few myself. But, with perhaps one or two exceptions, I don't think any can be called art books, or compilations of art photography.

What you hold in your hands is one of the exceptions. Peter Vincent's letterhead reads "Peter Vincent, Photographer." It's not a false claim. He doesn't have to go so far as to say "art photographer." That's evident in the work.

Not every photo in this book is an art photo. Many are simply comely portraits. Others are unquestionably works of art. But what I think might be even more important in this type of book is that Peter knows his rods and customs. This is crucial. Whether he's making artful pictures of them, or simply presenting them in more-than-competent photographs, he's showing you the real thing. These are not only excellent examples of rodding and customizing, but they also illustrate the wide diversity that exists in this field today. Page through this book and you will immediately understand how fun, wild, crazy, sleek, smooth, quaint, futuristic—yes, even artistic—rods and customs can be. Now if you could only hear, feel, and smell them as you watch them roar by . . . or even spray salt in your face.

—*Pat Ganahl*
Editor, The Rodder's Journal

INTRODUCTION: PHILIP E. LINHARES

The hot rod is a purely American expressive form. Emerging in the early twentieth century from California garages and backyards, tested on city streets, and proven on the dry lakebeds of Southern California, the hot rod is a complex symbol of American ingenuity and social meaning. Its younger cousin, the custom car, improves upon postwar American automotive design and evolved as an eloquently sensual boulevard cruiser. Nostalgia for our passing twentieth century objects and rituals has ushered the hot rod and custom car to a new prominence on the American scene.

Nostalgia can range from superficial motives to honored tradition. The former, superficial motives, might be the yearnings for a lost childhood or symptomatic of a second one, represented by jukebox sock hops, vintage rock 'n' roll music, and local "graffiti night" cruises. The latter, tradition, respects the accomplishments of generations of serious, inventive racers: Ab Jenkins, Bill Burke, Barney Navarro, Stu Hilborn, and Alex Xydias then; Al Teague, Don Vesco, and Tom Burkland now, among many others past and present.

Establishing builder's traditions were Sam and George Barris, Gene Winfield, and the Ayala Brothers, to name but a few; today, Barris and Winfield remain to observe Boyd Coddington, Pete Chapouris, Roy Brizio, Steve Moal, and Sam Foose extending our ideas of how a car should look and perform. And in their midst are the privateers: designers, producers, and entrepreneurs including Blackie Gejeian, John D'Agostino, Kent Fuller, Tom Prufer, Ron Covell, Chip Foose, and Vern Tardel, all contributing in their unique ways to further this American synthesis of art, design, engineering, and craftsmanship as an expression of our particular culture.

Actually, its been called a subculture, but the participants in this phenomenon couldn't care less. We, gatekeepers of the cultural institutions who decree what is and what is not art (or at least what is good or bad art, and publish arguments to prove it) have recently focused on the hot rod and custom car as exhibition material. From major museums to significant automotive beauty contests such as the Concours at Pebble Beach, hot rods and customs have been presented to both appreciative and unimpressed audiences.

Part of hot rods' problem is their humble beginning, and the fact that they are hybrids, cobbled-up mixes of nonpedigreed parts, which, quite often, outperform their superiors. Premature judgment does not consider the genesis of the thoroughbreds . . . but, didn't W.O. Bentley, Enzo Ferrari, Sidney Allard, and Colin Chapman exhibit some hot rodder–like vision and ingenuity? Let's give Steve Moal and Chip Foose a few years to clarify this relationship.

As a hot rodder myself, my idea of a great time is this: getting up at 4 A.M. on a mid-August morning, firing up the '35 Ford roadster, and meeting the Santa Rosa guys at the Cordelia truckstop at 6 A.M.; driving through Sacramento and up the Sierra foothills with the sun reflecting off our windshields; stopping for a lunch of chicken-fried steak and gravy at Boomtown, out of Reno; charging on in midday across the Nevada desert, stopping for gas

and coffee every two hours (the '29 roadsters have small gas tanks); trading cars on the way, happy to get back in the comfy '35 after guiding a cramped, bumpy '29 roadster up the road; stopping for more gas and snacks at Who-Knows-Where, Nevada; and cruising into Wendover an hour before sunset, past the high-dollar street rods parked in front of the casinos, and watching the guys standing out in front rush past the nice, painted cars to check out our bug-spattered, primered, flathead-powered beaters. And the best is yet to come: The Bonneville Salt Flats are just around the bend.

For many, Bonneville is the ultimate destination. A vast, treeless, pure white expanse of salt, it is inhospitable at first glance. You don't have to be a race driver to feel the adrenaline rush. But the inhospitality of the environment is quickly transformed under the shade pavilions in the pits. There you are, surrounded by racers, mechanics, helpers, and enthusiasts. Stand in the shade, stay out of the way of the workers and you are welcome to witness amazing feats of mechanical skill performed on some of the most spectacular, exotic, and fastest automobiles on earth. Soon enough you hear the sound of Al Teague's B/Fuel streamliner ricocheting off the distant mountains, and see the black Number 76 car streak across the salt at more than 300 miles per hour. It is good to be here then.

Peter Vincent spends lots of time at Bonneville, Muroc, and Paso Robles, too. He understands the visual language of the cars, and knows how to use a camera in a way that captures the essence of these machines in their natural, rightful habitat. His empathy with the landscape and environments in his photographs is deeply felt and clearly expressed in each image. Ultimately, the photographs, works of art in themselves, affirm the beauty and depth of their subjects as well.

It took jazz, another purely American expressive form, many years to gain wide public acceptance as "art"; it took photography quite some time too. Perhaps early in the twenty-first century, we will decide to accept these unique automobiles as works of art. Peter Vincent's photographs help to show us why.

Jeff Aldrich's 1929 Ford Roadster photographed at Muroc.

—*Philip E. Linhares*
Chief Curator of Art
The Oakland Museum of California

Note: *Philip E. Linhares and Michael Dobrin were co-curators on the Oakland Museum of California Exhibit "Hot Rods and Customs: The Men and Machines of California's Car Culture," which ran from September 1996 to January 1997. This landmark exhibit explored and provided examples of the unique American cultural phenomenon of hot rods, custom cars, and the men who created and built them.*

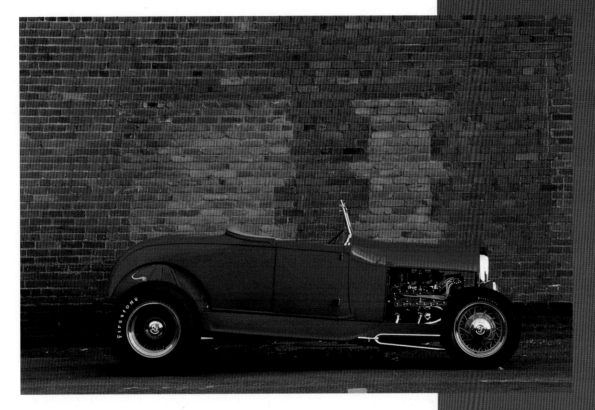

Gary Harms spent five years collecting parts for this '28 Ford roadster, which is based on a '32 frame. The car was completed in 1991, and with Gary's dedication to period authenticity, it is almost all Ford. Probably the only non-Ford parts on this car are the Hartford shocks, Ross steering box, the Vertex magneto, and the alternator, which is now housed inside an original generator housing. The engine is the classic 3/8 by 3/8 flathead, which gives it 296 ci. The flathead is dressed with rare Evans heads and three-deuce intake manifold topped with three Stromberg 97s, and backed by a '39 Ford transmission filled with Zephyr gears. A '48 Ford torque tube was reworked in the rear to match up with the Model A quick-change. Ford brakes all around help slow down the roadster's 16-inch Kelsey Hayes wheels, which were widened in back to 10 inches. Firestone dirt trackers, front and rear, meet the pavement. The roadster is beautifully detailed, and all of the work, with the exception of the top, interior, chrome work, and body metal finishing, is Gary's, right down to the louvers in the hood and deck lid. He has his own press.

THE TRADITIONAL
HOT ROD

This group of hot rods was photographed at Bonneville in 1999 one evening as the racing was ending for the day. Many of these cars show up every year and add to the "originality" of the era. They also add to the landscape, or the landscape adds to them. Which it is, I'm not really sure, but it works.

The "traditional" hot rod has been part of the American cultural scene since the 1920s, when the first Model T was stripped down for racing. From that time, the hot rod has been reformed and redesigned as new automotive models were introduced. These stripped down models were not called "hot rods" before World War II, but the conceptual form was there. The culture was formed far ahead of the recognizable term.

In hot rod culture, the term "traditional" can have different connotations. For some, traditional refers to the historical time period in which the hot rod was first built. For others, traditional involves the style and the way the hot rod is built, regardless of when it was constructed. For the purpose of this book, we are following the second definition, that which emphasizes style. The problem with this definition is that there were many styles, each denoting a time period in the history of the hot rod. If one were to remain "true" to the style, nothing out of that time period could be used on the car. For instance, a four-bar front suspension setup or billet aluminum wheels on a 1950s style hot rod would be out of place. It doesn't mean that four-bar setups or billet wheels can't be used on a hot rod, just that they shouldn't be used on one that is trying to remain true to an earlier period.

Pete Eastwood lists this T as being in the 1911–1927 year range, and it is a Model T racer. The 1919 Model T engine was built by Jerry Sherman with a Model A crankshaft, special cam, and Sherman Super Fire flathead pistons. There is a BBI-Carter carburetor and a Bosch ignition, along with owner-built headers. The modified T suspension sits on a 95-inch wheel based frame with 23-inch Buffalo wheels and 30x3.5-inch tires. This single-seat racer has a hand-built cowl and seat, a 1911 "torpedo" hood (which is 2 inches longer than other models) with the owner and Mother Nature adding the Krylon paint and natural "patina" to the car. This T racer is typical of early dirt-track racers. Ts like this first showed up at races like the 1911 and 1912 Santa Monica Road Races, where H. J. Charles raced his in the "light car class." By the late teens and early 1920s more sophisticated Ts were being built for the dirt tracks. This car was photographed at the Muroc Reunion in 1997, out on the dirt. It felt right visually. Pete raced this at the Auburn Hill Climb and the Visalia Motorsports Races, as well as showing up at the River City Reliability Run for the 100-plus-mile jaunt up into the Southern California mountains. Absolutely cool, and folks, this is what it's all about.

Pete has been involved with hot rods and the automotive culture all of his life, including the classics and restoration, especially involving vintage race cars. He bought his first car at 11 with a loan of $150 from his father for a garage full of "stuff" (parts and pieces), which he turned into a Model T. He sold enough of the "leftover" parts to pay back the loan to his father and end up with a profit of around $25. He is known for his craftsmanship and overall ability in both the hot-rod and classic car arenas. There is a definite aesthetic and finesse that comes through in all his work. If you ever had a chance to look at this Model T closely, you would have noticed the workmanship and detail. These cars were really the first platform for the creation of the hot rod, except that in their days and the time period in which they were built, they were called "go" (gow) jobs. He also mentioned that Ted Stirling, or the Stirling Garage, was really the first place someone could go to have a "hot rod" built. They had a formula for putting together the Model Ts that included dropped axles, high-performance engines, etc. There is probably a wealth of history and information in this subject area alone.

The traditional hot rods presented in this chapter are a compendium of styles from the 1920s to the present. Period overlaps are difficult to categorize accurately, but they are roughly sequenced in time and according to style. To further complicate the issue and dialogue, there is the debate of whether the car should be called a "hot rod" or a "street rod," with the latter being built for comfort and street driving rather than for performance or racing. The debate as to what is a hot rod and what is a street rod has fueled conversations for the past 20 or so years, and many people I have interviewed hold strong opinions about the difference. While it is hard to pin down, to many a hot rod is race-bred and built for performance. A hot rod, especially a traditional one, does not move into the creature comfort realm; it doesn't have air conditioning, power windows, or power seats, although this is under debate by many. A "look," or an aesthetic, is part of the defining nature of the traditional hot rod. Most of the seasoned veterans of the hot rod world can tell you in a minute whether or not a certain car fits into the traditional hot rod category. The decision comes from a "gut" reaction or instinctive feeling. I too have employed this method in defining and organizing the contents of this book.

With the advent of the National Street Rod Association (NSRA) in the early 1970s, and different magazines, such as *Street Rodder*, versus the early original magazines, such as *Hot Rod*, *Rod & Custom*, or *Hop Up*, the street rod side of the equation has risen to its current popularity, which we discuss in a later chapter.

The lineage of the hot rod comes from racing. The evolution of styles centers on a "form follows function" concept. Cars were modified to make them go faster by cutting down the wind

drag and improving the power-weight ratio. Fenders were removed to reduce wind resistance and weight. Tops and windshields were chopped, and some roadster windshields were actually removed for the racing event. Louvers were added for cooling and to release built-up air pressure from under the car. It became important to keep low to the ground as the speed increased, and racers realized the impact of the air on the car. Small, narrow front tires helped reduce wind drag. With the focus on racing, the car needed more rear traction, hence, larger tires, which also increased the effective gear ratios needed to reach increasingly higher speeds.

Acceleration, rather than top speed, has also been an important part of the hot rod culture, so there has been a lot of experimentation with the rear tire size in relation to traction and proper gearing for acceleration. Cars were lowered in the front to help reduce frontal area and to also help keep the car on the ground. Nerf bars were lighter than spring steel bumpers and possibly evolved from rear push bars used to get race cars started or pushed off the line in land speed racing and early drag racing.

Engines, beginning with the early four-cylinders up to later V-8s, kept getting larger displacements, with higher compression and more horsepower. High compression ratios, made possible by yesterday's high-octane gasoline, created a very traditional sound that comes from a performance engine and exhaust system. The American V-8 has become an icon in itself and the sound, particularly when unmuffled, is music to many ears and the bane of others.

Ford parts, such as transmissions and rear ends, were adaptable, cheap, and readily available, as were the old Ford cars. Drivetrain parts were exchangeable from year to year. Hydraulic brakes from the newer models up to 1948 were easily adaptable to all the earlier Fords, which were originally equipped with mechanical brakes. The Ford V-8 flathead engine was used extensively up until the mid-1950s. Speed equipment manufacturers were able to offer special parts because of this interchangability. In 1955, Chevrolet introduced its small-block V-8, which has remained popular over the years for the same reasons: availability and interchangability. Speed equipment could also be mass-produced for the Chevrolet small-block in quantities large enough to make it profitable for manufacturers and affordable for the average hot rodder.

With racing as the prime imperative, speed became the prime directive, and nothing was left on the car that would hinder its speed. Everything that defines a hot rod today has come from racing tradition, although the hot rod has also been stylized and altered through the years for a visual and visceral impact. What remains interesting is that certain traits have become constant, and these traits are the ones that keep traditional hot rodding within certain realms.

To get back to the original questions, why is a hot rod a hot rod, and what is the difference between a hot rod and a street rod? If you ask 10 different experts, you will probably get 10 different answers. For most, a hot rod doesn't have air conditioning, power windows, or other plush creature comforts, while a street rod could. A traditional hot rod, to many, must have an I-beam or tubular front axle. This seems to be one of the major items in consideration and if you ask why, many will tell you that it is because that is the way it has been throughout hot rod history.

I believe the criteria are also visual, and have to do with the overall aesthetics of a "traditional hot rod." A number of elements point in this direction, and most of them serve functionality. It's that "form follows function" thing again. Some hot rod criteria: big tires on the back, smaller (probably narrow) tires on the front, louvers, quick-change rear ends, Buick or early Ford brake drums, nerf bars, chopped tops or windshields, flames, scallops, early style pinstriping (Von Dutch or Tommy the Greek), Stewart Warner gauges, Bell steering wheels, four-speed transmissions, Naughahyde interiors (simple), Moon tanks, carburetors or maybe Hilborn fuel injection, Roots-type blowers, dual pipes, headers, steel wheels, Halibrand wheels, American Torque Thrust wheels, ETIII's, and the list goes on and on. But it's not just parts, it's definitely how all of these elements are put together. It's the "stance," or how the car sits on the ground. Is it raked, that is, lower in the front than in the back? What it really comes down to is the demeanor, the simplicity, and straight forwardness of construction. If the car is nasty, a little edgy, and in your face, it probably is a hot rod.

The hot rod has a purely American aesthetic that comes from the roots and the tradition. A hot rod is essentially created for performance. Whether it be for actual racing or street performance, it really doesn't matter, as I have ridden in many hot rods that would do well on the dry lakes or the drag strip, but had probably never been run on either. They had been driven extensively on the street, but they are really closer to the racing side of the equation than they are to the comfort side. They definitely got my attention. Uniquely, a hot rod can also be a non-race-oriented car, with an engine and horsepower rating suited to street use, but it is still a hot rod because of the way everything is put together and the way it fits into the hot rod concept. This has been debated long and hard by many. Again, while there are many opinions on the definition of a hot rod, I'll show some visual viewpoints and perspectives in this chapter. Remember, it isn't any one thing that makes a hot rod, it is the combination in which elements are put together.

People from different generations, and different regions of the country, developed a hot rod aesthetic reflecting those influences. The magazines, published mainly out of Southern California, passed this look on to anyone and everyone who entered the culture through their pages. I know people who were greatly influenced by cars in the 1940s, while other were influenced by cars in the 1950s, 1960s, or even a combination. Fads come and go but the classics endure. The traditional hot rod is something that will remain through all of the new styles. While some of the new may evolve into a classic look itself, only time will tell how the hot rod culture evolves.

Several individuals have become taste masters and have defined, or redefined, hot rods through their creations. Vern Tardel is into late 1940s and early 1950s-styled, flathead-powered hot rods, and the cars he puts together are definitely what I would consider traditional hot rods. Tardel is a master at putting together and using the interchangability of early Ford parts to build an early style hot rod. In another definitive style, Bill Vinther is into the late 1950s, early 1960s style of hot rods. I'd say his cars also belong in the traditional hot rod realm. Tardel's cars will probably have tall skinny bias-ply tires and original steel wheels or possibly Kelsey-Hayes wire wheels; Vinther's cars might be shod with dirt-track rear tires and polished magnesium wheels, and they are extensively lowered, especially in the front. Tardel's would be running a flathead V-8, while Vinther's would run a 327-ci Chevrolet small-block with as much compression and cam as he could comfortably run on today's gas. It has to be a 327, or maybe a 283, but probably not one of the newer 350-ci small-blocks. Yet, both cars might favor quick-change rear ends, chopped tops, Stewart-Warner–type gauges, louvers, or all of the above.

You won't find a piece of billet aluminum on either builder's car, as it wouldn't fit the "style" or period of history that they revere. Both are very conscious of what works and what doesn't work with each period style. They won't mix periods. Both were influenced heavily by the time period in which they grew up working on cars and hot rods. I have talked with many hot rodders who claim that a certain car caught their attention and sparked a passion that drew them into the hot rod culture. Most people attribute their personal interest to certain periods of expression characterized in the 1940s, 1950s, or early 1960s.

Young hot rodders today understand the historical vocabulary and are very conscious of the correct lineage of parts needed to make a car period perfect. They struggle with the limited availability of parts. What we found readily and inexpensively available in the 1950s and 1960s is much harder to find nowadays. They are very resourceful and are willing to experiment and learn about the "old" ways. Old magazines and old-timers shape their aesthetic. Their positive energy is infusing the culture, and an excitement and energy that had been slipping away is now being reintroduced. These retro-rodders are into the life and culture full tilt, and they are not worried about getting the cars a little dirty or driving them on the open road. This is what hot rodding is.

As they grow into the culture, they have to be careful not to lose sight of the historical perspective. For a fine example, Brett Reed showed up at Muroc and Bonneville in 1999 with a "right-on" early styled '32 Ford highboy. He is now converting the roadster into a full-blown Bonneville race car. This is something he is doing for the passion of it. It fits into what the hot rod culture is about in a historical sense. There were some hot rods at the first Muroc Reunion in 1996 that I could not tell from the original older hot rods, and race cars that were there from the early dry lakes era. These were new hot rods and it was probably, for many of us, a first look at some of the new energy that was happening out there. The younger hot rodders were enjoying it, and in fact, we all were, dirt and all.

Another car that I kept seeing at Muroc and Bonneville was a '29 roadster owned by Jeff Archer, out of Half Moon Bay, California. This car belonged there, it looked right, and it fit in a very subtle and cool "sitting in the background" way. There is no "power parking" (that is, jockeying for a prominent parking place) at the dry lakes, or at Bonneville. These cars were right at home with the other more well-known hot rods at the first Muroc Reunion, such as Bruce Meyer's early Bonneville Pierson Brother's coupe, Jim "Jake" Jacobson's yellow '34 coupe, or Pete Chapouris' '34 coupe, the *California Kid*. The latter two are now owned by Jerry Slover, who bought the original Pete & Jake's Hot Rod Parts business. All these cars embody the hot rod culture and are true to various periods within the culture.

The true beauty of the hot rod culture is that there are what I would call guidelines, but no ironclad rules. One can build a hot rod to personal satisfaction, which is part of the reason there is so much creative energy out there. The hot rod is a carefully thought-out vehicle of personal expression and individuality. Creativity, focus, and dedication come together to produce something meaningful. In a broader sense, the hot rod is an American art form. The conceptual similarities are there.

As I open the hot rod to this conceptual area, I expect debate to follow. I define "hot rod" as an automobile that has been stripped for performance and built to be "somewhat" race ready, or built for performance, particularly land speed racing or drag racing. This definition has always been debated and tossed around. Some believe it to include only certain years, such as pre-1949 cars; others open up the years a little more, but hold to the concept. For me, it really is a question about attitude, and by that I mean the car's

This is a '26 Ford Bobtail T Racer that Don Small has recently raced in the Auburn Hill Climb, Visalia Motorsports Races, and the 2000 Antique Nationals, where he took the trophy for the T Bracket. The '26 T four-cylinder engine is running a C crank and rods, full oil pressure, and a Laurel Roof eight-Valve overhead. Don runs a 4:10 T rear end with a Model T transmission and Nash three-speed with overdrive. There is a dropped front axle and cross-member with a shortened frame that has been "kicked up" 5 inches. The 30x3.5-inch Buffalo wire wheels are shod with Firestone tires, and the car uses a Franklin sprint car steering box. The body is patterned after the old Ed Winfield and Vern Gerber "Bobtails," with the grille and radiator from a Whippet. The very short seat has red leather from an old Jaguar. The similarities to traditionally built hot rods are there in the construction and concept. The car was photographed at the Muroc Reunion in 1998.

attitude. I have a problem defining a car as a hot rod if it drifts too far into the creature comfort realm—power windows, power seats, or air conditioning. Even then, I will make exceptions if the attitude is right. One of the great things about building a hot rod is that there aren't any rules, but there are perceived visual and functional guidelines.

The second part of the equation is the term "traditional." What this means, as stated by the *Twentieth Century Webster's Dictionary*, is: "the delivery of opinions, doctrines, practices, rites, and customs from generation to generation by oral communication," or that which is customary or conventional. Are we saying that there are no rules in the hot rod culture, but that there are stringent guidelines and conventions? Should we be free to create what we want, as long as what we create resides within the framework of the hot rod culture? Just don't get too far outside the box. We return to the classic "form follows function" aesthetic in defining a hot rod, especially when we are talking about a traditional hot rod.

Another point that separates the hot rod from the street rod is that you have to tinker with a hot rod. You have to know what makes the car work and not work. These are performance vehicles, and they can be touchy at times. They need care, knowledge, and much more maintenance than the average car. Street rods push a little more in the family car direction and are more reliable and more comfortable. One is not any better than the other, and it really comes down to a matter of individual choice. I have seen many people get into something that is high performance, and lose interest or become frustrated because of the care it required. I also know many people who are not interested in traveling very far in something that isn't comfortable to sit in for long periods. The rest is for you to debate, define, and decide.

The photos in this chapter have been set up in a chronological order involving style rather than the actual time or year of construction. While "bob-tailed" Model T speedsters have not traditionally been called hot rods, I believe they should be. They were some of the first American-made cars to be modified, stripped down, and hopped up. These cars were showing up at the dirt tracks in 1911 or 1912, or at the Santa Monica Road Race in the "light car class." Two of the recent cars, owned by Pete Eastwood and Don Small, were photographed at Muroc during the Southern California Timing Association (SCTA) land speed trials held at Edwards Air Force Base in the late 1990s. This supports the feeling that they should really be placed in the traditional hot rod chapter. They are, in my view, hot rods; by definition, they fit the genre.

Introduction into late 1930s and Early 1940s Hot Rods

After the era of the Model T hot rods came the Model As, built by Ford from 1928 to 1931. Originally equipped with flathead four-cylinder engines, Model As were light, cheap, and in the 1930s, plentiful, as were four-cylinder engines and flathead V-8s. A good example of an early hot rod would be a '28 or '29 roadster body on a Model A frame, with tall skinny tires on Kelsey-Hayes wire wheels or stock steel wheels. The engine would be either a hopped-up four-cylinder Model A or B motor or an early flathead V-8 Ford. The windshield could be slanted back, and the headlights mounted low, as styling for that time period was in the functional "pull it off to race" arena. Many of these early hot rods had no fenders, hoods, or anything that added weight. If they did have such "accessories," the parts were easily removed on race day.

George Williams' '26 Model T roadster is a copy of pre–World War II dry lakes cars. The car has had many different engines in it; Ts, As, Chevrolets, and Oldsmobiles, all four-cylinders. It also had its share of Ford V-8 flatheads, which is what it has now. It is a '40 Ford V-8-60, followed by a '37 Ford three-speed transmission and a Ford "banjo" rear end. George narrowed the Model T body 9 inches, and he is running 16-inch Kelsey-Hayes wheels with 7.50 tires on the rear and motorcycle tires on the front. The suspension is all early Ford.

Most of the cars in this group tend toward the early dry lakes look, and actually look as if they could have been racers from this era. Some of the younger hot rodders are definitely getting the look down with some of their recently built cars. We started seeing some of these at the first Muroc Reunion (located on Edwards Air Force Base, which is a dry lake bed in California) in the mid-1990s. I have included some photographs taken at that time. At the Muroc Reunion, I spent as much time back in the hot rod parking area as I did in the pits, and I was supposed to be helping crew on a race car. Nonetheless, what I saw was exciting, and seeing these cars on the dry lake setting was appropriate and visually perfect. The setting and natural landscape lends itself to authentic-looking hot rod photographs, as this is where the hot rod culture started. There were not many "billet" cars or fairground cruisers out on the lakebed, but there were some great examples of traditional hot rods. The images should speak for themselves. It feels right, and the light, which all photographers covet, is fantastic.

I ran into Steve "Carps" Carpenter, driving Drew Pietsch's '28–'29 Dodge roadster at Muroc during the 2000 reunion. The dust was up and everyone was having a grand time between the gusts of wind. The photographs were worth the effort as the time period could be pre–World War II, without much imagination, especially if they had been in black and white instead of color. Drew's roadster is running a '42-21A Merc flathead with a '39 gearbox and a '41 Ford Deluxe rear end. The chassis and suspension are '31 Model A with '28 Chevy steering. The car runs '40 Ford 16-inch wheels on the front with B-41 Lincoln rims on the rear. This "shorty" roadster is "rattle can" painted and the interior is from "Auntie Mabel's" couch, which is missing a couple of cushions. These guys are having far too much fun.

This photograph was taken at Muroc in 2000 at the reunion on Sunday morning, just before leaving to catch a plane back to Idaho. I didn't get all the specs on the "shorty" or a name, but I liked the car and it fits in this era and out on the dry lakes. It looks like it belongs there.

Mike Bishop and Bill Ross at the 50th Bonneville Speedweek anniversary, posing beside their respective rides. Mike with his late 1940s authentically styled '29 Ford highboy roadster, and Bill with his "soon to be painted emerald green" full custom '46 Ford convertible, were out on the salt for the celebration.

HOT RODS IN THE POSTWAR YEARS

By Mike Bishop

The primary forms of hot rod sport prior to World War II were dirt-track and dry lakes racing. These interests continued as the principal influences on hot rod design and construction after the war and into the mid-1950s, in spite of the burgeoning interest in two new forms of competition—drag racing and road racing. Drag racing would exert its influence in a big way before the decade was over. Road racing hot rods, however, quickly evolved along distinctly European lines, and soon had little to do with the general hot rod community. Dirt-track hot rods likewise metamorphosed rapidly into sophisticated, sleek race cars, stranding the lovable track roadster long before it ceased pleasing race fans.

"Rake," the down-in-front stance that came to define the West Coast look, was in increasing evidence. In most cases it was achieved with tall tires in the rear and short ones in front ("big 'n' littles)." The reason for the disparate tire sizes was hot rod simple and practical: The tall rear tires provided a higher effective final-drive ratio for higher top speed, and the shorter front tires created an increased attack angle to improve stability at high speed. The look carried over from the dry lakes to the street, for both practical reasons and appearance. With the majority of lakes-raced hot rods also serving as transportation, the taller "gearing" reduced engine wear and improved fuel economy. And while there could be an easy argument made for the look being a simple matter of form following function, the popularity of the rake probably has as much to do with the aggressive stance it provides. It's still a great look.

One of the more significant pieces of improved hardware in the immediate postwar period, the dropped axle, would come on slowly at first, but as the 1940s drew to a close it was clearly becoming a must-have piece. By the mid-1950s a "Dago" axle from one of Ed Stewart's speed-shop clients, or any of the several other remanufacturers stretching and reshaping the forged beams, was standard hot-rod fare on an open-wheel car.

The Deuce chassis emerged as the first choice for a large number of hot rodders after the war. Model A-based A-V-8s from the 1930s, however, were still numerous and remained popular because of the considerably lower cost, compared to a Deuce. Even then, a '32 roadster was a relatively scarce model. Only a little more than 12,000 roadsters were built for the entire worldwide market.

But there was an alternative to the Deuce roadster body: '32 Ford tudor and fordor sedans that had soldiered on as transportation during World War II were rapidly being put out to pasture as new car production resumed in 1946. These cast-off sedans provided ready-made hot-rod chassis platforms for handsome and relatively plentiful '28–'29 roadster bodies. This resulted in one of hot rodding's best-loved hybrids, the Model A on Deuce rails.

Street rodders and others new to the hobby today have difficulty imagining why anyone would scrap the sheet metal from a perfectly good '32 Ford tudor or fordor sedan just to harvest the chassis. Remember that at the time, even three-window coupes were just beginning to be accepted as legitimate hot rods, and a tudor or fordor sedan wasn't even a contender. They were just used cars. Consider, too, that a good unmodified Deuce roadster would command $300–$500, while an equivalent fordor was worth $100 and a complete '29 Model A roadster would bring another $100. Hot rodding was still very much a matter of going as fast as one could with very little money. The A-on-Deuce approach meant more dollars were available for speed equipment and machine work—provided one was willing to trade the Deuce roadster dream for a bit more speed.

Before the 1940s ended, the open-wheel roadster would begin to decline relative to the growth of the movement, more from necessity than desire, as cheap and plentiful coupes, sedans, and closed-cab pickups were hot rodded into respectable and suitable rides.

—Mike Bishop

Opposite
John Carambia's '29 Ford roadster is a classic example of a late 1930s through 1940s hot rod, especially one of the dry lakes versions. The roadster body, last registered in 1947, was an old hot rod at one time; John pieced it together and put it on a '32 frame. The stock B four-cylinder engine has a Winfield head and dual carburetor setup. The '32 frame kept the '32 B transmission and the '32 rear end. The wheel combination is 18-inch straight spoke wheels in front, with 17-inch bent spoke wheels in back.

I photographed this old drag racer at Muroc during the 1998 reunion along with Don Small's T speedster. They both looked like naturals out on the dirt. The Number 4 race car is running a Cragar head on a Model B block along with a '48 truck transmission and open driveline. The rear-end differential is a Cyclone quick-change, and it has Lincoln front brakes. The paint is over 40 years old, and the word is that this car ran the drags often in the 1950s and 1960s with a four-banger engine. It is somewhat of a mystery car other than that. It just looked right.

Steve Beck's '29 roadster pickup is running an AB flathead V-8 with milled heads for an increased compression ratio of 6:1. Steve ran down an original Isky 116 track cam from the 1940s, and added an early Edelbrock "regular" two-pot manifold. The transmission is a Zephyr-geared (26-tooth) '39 Ford with a narrowed '40 4:41 Ford rear end. The windshield has been raked back and the stance is helped with a dropped '34 axle. The roadster runs 16-inch Kelsey Hayes wheels all around with 5.50 front tires and 7.00 tires on the rear.

23 The Traditional Hot Rod

Dave Lukkari does get around with his Model A, which is powered by an Ardun-headed and S.Co.T.-blown 262-cid '51 Mercury. I have seen this car at the Muroc Reunions and various Bonneville events. This "shorty" roadster pickup is a natural of the era. The Zora Arkus Duntov-designed hemispherical heads are sculptures in themselves, as are the S.Co.T. blower and Stromberg carburetors. I actually used one of these blowers in an art exhibit I curated once as original sculpture, right next to a "finned" magnesium Halibrand V-8 quick-change. They are beautiful pieces and represent true classic versions of functional American machine art. Seeing Lukkari's roadster out on the lakes, or at Bonneville, brings about some of the same feelings.

Julio Hernandez's seriously chopped and channeled '30 Model A coupe also looks perfect out on the dirt of Muroc. I photographed the car at the 2000 reunion as part of a group of cars built by younger hot rodders and custom builders. The '54 Chevy in the foreground is Willow Kirk's, but Julio's A definitely is a low "lakes"-style coupe; it's only belt-high when you are standing next to the car. He is running a Mercury flathead hooked to a '39 Ford transmission and a Ford 8-inch rear end. Julio stitched the tucked and rolled interior, and Fabian Valdez laid out the white scallops on the flat black paint.

Far right
Todd Walling and Keith Tardel put this early-styled '27 T roadster together as a drivable and functional ride. Todd drove it to Bonneville to attend Speedweek 2000 with the Tardel group. He says it's probably one of his most dependable cars, which says a lot about Tardel's early Ford and flathead engine knowledge. The 59AB block has three Stromberg 97's on an Offenhauser manifold with Offy heads and a Mercury crankshaft. The '39 Ford transmission hooks up to a '46 Ford rear end.

Jim Stroupe lists this car as a '27 Ford phaeton/modified. The hopped up DOHC 2000-cc Alfa engine powers this modified down the highway through an aluminum five-speed transmission and a Model A Halibrand quick-change rear end. He had Roy Brizio build the car, which is indeed, a collection of rare and desirable parts. The early unpolished 15-inch Halibrand mags and Firestone tires, the Kinmont brakes, Roto-Flo shocks, the Model A Halibrand quick-change, and the '32 Plymouth front axle all combine to help showcase the intricate craftsmanship that went into putting this modified together. The cut-down phaeton body was narrowed 8 inches and painted "no moon" blue by Darryl Hollenbeck. Sid Chavers stitched the old-style pleated red leather interior and Stewart Warner gauges fill the '32-type custom dash to complete the early look. The Alfa engine and the five-speed transmission obviously come from a newer time period, but, it is a well-thought-out and beautiful rendition of the period in a visual sense.

37 The Traditional Hot Rod

Jim Kitchen had a roadster he used to take on some of the southern California reliability runs, such as the River City Reliability Run, but he parted it out to build a Bonneville race car, right down to the frame. He sold everything but the body in 165 minutes. This two-door highboy sedan is what he takes to the salt. I've seen it there almost every year, but you can't let the "Mercury" emblem on the back throw you. It's probably a Ford, but he says it's a Merc. Who am I to say different? He thoroughly "salt-flocked" the car out there in 1999, which probably had something to do with the pond you had to drive through to get out to the pits and race-course. He should have a "don't do this at home" sticker on the windshield. The tall, skinny original Halibrands and tires are the perfect combination. Jim does things the way he wants to, and believes it all should be enjoyed.

Bob Stewart's '32 roadster has history, as it was built and owned by his father, Ed "Axle" Stewart, who earned the nickname for his reworking I-beam axles into the "Dago" dropped axle. Bob earned the nickname "Li'l Axle" by working in his father's shop doing machine work and custom block and head porting. The roadster was disassembled in 1959 for a complete rebuild and it remained that way for 28 years. Bob finished the rebuild in 1989, and has since put over 10,000 miles per year on the odometer. Other than the original Stewart Dago axle, one of the things that always catches people's eyes are the large Stewart Warner gauges. They have been called "North Island gauges," as they came from the U.S. Navy's North Island repair facility in San Diego. They were also called "lunch box gauges," leaving one to silently ponder the method of acquisition. Bob refers to them as "old man gauges," helpful for old eyes. I spent some time looking at the roadster at Bonneville in 1992, one night after talking with him for a while. This was Bob's first visit back at the salt since 1956, when he raced a '34 three-window coupe with his father. We finally got together at Pleasanton to photograph his '32. I have since lamented the fact that I did not photograph the roadster at Bonneville in 1992, but it also was the year that the salt was covered by 3 inches of water. The roadster is a beautiful and traditional period piece that Bob brought back together true to its earlier heritage. The roadster was driven on the streets in the 1940s, and in 1947 it ran 138.46 miles per hour at El Mirage. The car also saw some drag strip time in the early 1950s. The roadster is now running a 296-inch flathead with forged pistons, a Potvin 3/8 camshaft, rare Evans heads, and a 3-2 manifold with Stromberg 48's. The headers are original Belond units that flow back into 28-inch glasspacks. The transmission is a '41 Lincoln overdrive unit and the rear end is a Halibrand quick-change with 9-inch axles. The Lincoln/Bendix brakes work as good as anything that could have been chosen for stopping power. Bob has held true to the car's original heritage and history, and he kept it in the family in a beautiful and authentic rendition.

Chris Jory showed up at Mark Morton's River City Reliability Run in 1999 with this Deuce roadster highboy after a long drive down from Portland, Oregon (the Reliability Run being in Riverside, California). Three things really caught my attention. The first was the beautiful dark green paint and the chopped tan folding top. But then there were the original-looking side curtains, which I am sure made the trip down from Portland in December a little more enjoyable and comfortable. The third thing was period-perfect authenticity to everything about the roadster. It is very subtle and arresting, which says a lot about the choice of color. Chris is running a '65 Chevy 265-ci engine with an original Duntov cam, three Stromberg 97s on an Offenhauser intake and Spaulding Flamethrower ignition. The transmission is a '39 Ford with Zephyr gears and the rear end is a '40 Ford with 9-inch axles. The wheels are '47 Mercury 15-inch steelies with 560 and 820 BFG Silvertown tires mounted on them. The steering is a 1955 F100 box mated to a 1940 Ford column and wheel, which matches the stock restored '40 Ford dash and gauges. Oxblood tucked and rolled upholstery adorns the interior. It all works, and it is a very authentic 1950s hot rod, with a drift toward the very early part of the decade if you discount the Chevy 265 engine.

It's worth mentioning that racers started using the new overhead-valve V-8 engines as soon as they were introduced in the factory-produced Detroit cars. Oldsmobile and Cadillac V-8s introduced in 1949 were the earliest choices available. Then the Chrysler Corporation introduced the hemispherical (hemi)-headed V-8 in the early 1950s. Before this, hot rodders had experimented with various aftermarket versions of the overhead-valve V-8, such as the very successful Ardun head conversion for the flathead Ford, but in general, many of them still relied on the flathead V-8. That is, they did until Chevrolet introduced the 265-cid small-block V-8 in 1955, which, with minor modifications, would fit anywhere a flathead would.

Some of the hot rodders continued to use the Olds, Cadillac, and Buick V-8s from GM and the Chrysler, Dodge, or DeSoto hemi overheads, as there was a large amount of aftermarket speed equipment available for most of these larger, more powerful engines. These were considered classic hot rod engine examples all through the 1950s. The Chevy small-block would became the natural, however, primarily because of its size and adaptability from year to year. The 265-, 283-, 302-, 307-, 327-, and the 350-inch engines had many interchangeable parts, and there were increasing numbers of them available. They were also easy to "hot rod" and increase the horsepower rating.

This roadster, owned by Tom Branch when I photographed it at the Muroc Reunion in 2000, has since been sold. The roadster was featured in the March 1952 issue of *Hop Up* magazine as the Eddie Dye car, and will probably be restored to that form. Eddie originally contacted Gil Ayala to do the construction, which ran up a total cost of $3,400 for the six months of labor that it took to finish it. The roadster, at that time, had a track nose and a full hood. Tom's version has a small-block Chevy engine with three deuces, a cut-down '32 grille shell and a different windshield from the original, which was a DuVall. I like it both ways. The original *Hop Up* article in 1952 didn't mention what engine, or anything about the drivetrain at all for that matter. As you can see from the photographs, Tom enjoyed the roadster as a driver and wasn't afraid of a little dirt. It's a hot rod, and now that it has been sold, Tom's new project has already been started. Don Orosco is the new owner and will probably restore it to its original state.

This Model T "Turtledeck" Chevy small-block–powered roadster was at the Muroc Reunion in 2000 with the occupants watching the races.

Robert William's *Eights & Aces* full-fendered and primered (forever) '32 Ford roadster at the first Muroc Reunion in 1996. Robert is a well-known artist with a hot-rod bent, and it shows in his choice of cars and the style they're built in.

Left

Ryan Mead crews on a roadster at Bonneville and drives this red '34 Ford pickup there every year from Billings, Montana. What caught my eye were the wire wheels with bias-ply Firestone wide white wall tires and the 276-ci DeSoto hemi engine with the four deuce carburetors. There is also the all-important stance, which is right on. The DeSoto engine is running a Clay Smith cam, and Ryan adapted a turbo 350 behind the hemi with an 8-inch Ford rear end mounted with a four-link and original spring setup to finish the drivetrain. The dropped front I-beam axle is also set up with an original spring and split wishbones and mounts to a '32 frame. Ryan started on this car when he was a freshman in high school and did all the work, including the 4-inch top chop and removing 12 inches from the bed's length. He also sprayed the Sherwin Williams Coca-Cola red paint. The interior has the original bench seat and Stewart Warner Wings gauges.

Bub Johnson's '29 Ford roadster pickup looks like it is a holdover from the '50s. The white tuck-and-roll upholstery works with the old red paint. The '48 286-ci Mercury flathead has been balanced, blueprinted, ported, and relieved with Edelbrock heads and a slingshot manifold. It has a '56 Merc spicer rear end and the frame as been Zed to get the back end down. The windshield and top are chopped, the bed has been shortened, and the rear fenders have been bobbed (shortened) with the addition of some Harley "coffin" taillights. He says it runs at 180 degrees in any weather, anywhere.

Jim "Jake" Jacobs' '28 Ford phaeton, or "tub," was one of the first budget-built hot rods to garner some respect and limelight. The '28, and Jake, helped bring some of the "fun" back into hot rodding, and he legitimized putting together a car from a bunch of leftover parts. Jake has it right, knows the history of the culture, and came up with a ride that is truly "right on the money," or lack there of, depending on how you want to look at it. He put everything together sometime around 1987–1988 and came up with a ride that took everybody back to that earlier

era. If you discount the 283 Chevy small-block, the rest of it could have come from the late 1940s, even the brush-applied red paint. Now, obviously, you have to look through the decoupaged *Hot Rod* magazine covers and pages to see it. No split wishbones, no dropped axle, just reverse-eyed springs and skinny, tall bias-ply wide white-walled tires to get the stance. The windshield has been chopped 3 inches and Pete Eastwood made the three-piece hood. It all sits on a '32 frame, which was narrowed 1-1/2 inches to better match the '28 Model A body.

The best way to start off this small eastern Oregon group is with a couple of photographs of four early-style hot rods. Bob Lick's black full-fendered '32 three-window coupe and his yellow 1940 standard coupe. Jim Lindsey's flamed '32 highboy roadster and last, but not least, Dale Wither's subtle, but very beautiful, black and traditional '40 deluxe coupe. These hot rods were photographed in Baker City, Oregon, some time ago late one summer evening. Bob has since sold the black three-window and Dale sold the black '40, but both remain classic examples of traditionally built hot rods.

This '32 coupe has been around for a while. Bob Lick built it, owned it for a while, and sold it to move on to other projects. Who owns it now, I'm not sure, but it is a classic example of a chopped, full-fendered three-window coupe. The body was chopped 2 inches with the center hinge on the door removed. The 276-ci '49 Mercury engine has been ported and relieved with a Clay Smith cam and Isky valve springs added. Early Evans heads, a four-deuce manifold, and a Vertex magneto finish out the engine compartment. A top-loader four-speed transmission carries the horsepower back to a V-8 Halibrand rear end. The original Kelsey Hayes wheels came from Bob's father's wrecking yard in 1962. The car took six years to finish and it was built on the farm with a stick welder and cutting torch. No patch-panels were used. Dale Withers sprayed the black acrylic enamel and Chuck Blanchard did the early tucked and rolled–style black upholstery. Another interesting piece of ingenuity is the '40 Ford column shift that operates the top loader four-speed.

Dale Withers owned this coupe for a period of time and sold it to, I believe, Rod Powell. It shows what you do, and don't need to do, to a '40 Ford coupe. The engine was replaced with a 283-ci Chevy hooked up to a stock 1940 Ford drivetrain, with a Columbia two-speed rear end. Dale lowered the car, found some original baby moon hubcaps, had the interior redone in classic mid-1950s T-bird black and white, and called it good, even down to the checked lacquer paint. The coupe is, quite simply, gorgeous just as it is.

Jim Lindsey always wanted a '32 Ford roadster, so when Dee Wescott produced a fiberglass roadster body, Jim sold his five-window coupe to purchase one of the first. The roadster was first completed in 1975 in the traditional highboy style. This roadster has seen times on the dragstrips of Oregon, such as Woodburn. Jim subscribes to a time when hot rodding was pure and simple. He rebuilt the roadster in 1993, keeping the original paint and redoing almost everything else. He added the flames and the V-8 Halibrand rear end, and cut the original top bows to craft a folding top that matches the chopped windshield. The roadster is all Ford, running a very healthy 289-cid small-block and a top-loader four-speed transmission. The Kelsey-Hayes wheels and Denman tires help keep the traditional look, especially when matched with the dropped and drilled I-beam axle and split wishbone setup.

Bob Lick picked up the '40 Ford coupe for $100, like in the old days, he says. Bob is a long-time hot rodder and he really leans toward the traditional in everything he builds. He also got into nostalgic drag racing, so this coupe was built with that in mind. Originally he was going to keep the car as close to old-style hot rod as possible, but changes have been made through the years in the quest for faster times on the strip. For a while, Bob was running a 383-ci Chevy small-block (350-inch block with a 400 crank) with a roller cam and all the necessary speed goodies to make it go fast. We rode around Baker City, Oregon, in it for an afternoon. It was lumpy, noisy, and absolutely fantastic. Bob was running a wide-ratio four-speed Muncie in it for a while, then switched to a Doug Nash five-speed. He also decided later to switch to a big-block Chevy and upgrade a few other things. At the time, the only body modifications were the small wheel tubs in the rear, just big enough to clear 10-inch slicks. I probably should have put this in the drag racing section, but I rode around in it that day as a hot rod, so that's where I put it.

Claude and Susan Freund previously owned this car in the 1970s. Russ Freund, their son, bought it in the 1990s from an intermediate owner after it had burned. This is Russ' first hot rod, and he built it from the ground up with an idea in mind of what it should look like. He obviously appreciates the traditional look, especially the look of the later 1950s. The very low stance, steel wheels without caps, wide whitewalls and notched slicks sticking out of the back fenders all tend toward this direction. Add to that a small-block Chevy with four deuces, straight pipes, chopped windshield and a rolled and pleated white interior by George Frank, and it definitely fits.

Far left top

I ran into Doug Anderson and his '31 Ford coupe, nicknamed *Boogie Woogie*, when he drove from New York for the 50th annual Bonneville Speedweek. I'm not sure there is anyone out there having more fun with hot rodding. His enthusiasm carries through, and when you realize his coupe chassis incorporates an NHRA and Bonneville legal roll bar and an optional bolt-in chrome moly "funny car" driver side cage assembly, you can believe his statement, "The car will be raced." He spent 8-1/2 years putting it all together in a style reminiscent of the late 1950s and early 1960s. The engine is a 10.5:1-compression 327-inch Chevy with an Offenhauser three-deuce manifold and a handmade progressive linkage setup smoothing out the Rochester carbs. He has some interesting pieces in the car, such as two Adirondack Redwing hockey pucks for motor mounts, a railroad crossing sign for the dashboard, a Montana 35-mile per hour sign for a transmission cover and two stop signs for bucket seat supports. Use what you have and "adapt." A good portion of this project was handmade from raw materials. And why the *Boogie Woogie* moniker? Simple, Doug says. He loves blues music almost as much as hot rods. It works.

Far left

Brent Housley's '32 Ford five-window coupe was originally bought in Scappose, Oregon, and it has never been registered more than 100 miles from there. The car was channeled in 1952 and chopped in the 1980s. The swing-out windshield and roll-down back window are still functional, and the car is all steel. Brent is running a 301-ci

Chevy small-block mated to a '39 Mercury transmission and a '40 Ford rear end. The top was chopped 4 inches, and the body is channeled 5 inches in front and 3 inches in the rear. The grille shell was sectioned 5 inches and the rear fenders have been bobbed. I've seen the car all over the Northwest and appreciate its real "old-time" authenticity. The black primer paint, flames, and pinstriping add to the overall 1950s look.

Left

Phil Huff's red oxide primered '32 five-window highboy coupe is traditional, especially with the Chrysler Firepower 354-ci hemi. It was one of the "low-keyed" cars driving through the pits at Bonneville during Speedweek 2000. A shop logo on the door, along with a few bullet holes, provided by an unknown Wyoming cowboy, that he decided not to fill are part of the ambiance. A column-shifted turbo 400 transfers the power from the Chrysler hemi to the Ford 9-inch rear end. Phil is enjoying the car, and doesn't spend time worrying about it when he's not behind the wheel.

Brett Reed is a rock and roller out of the Bay Area. He's also a committed hot rodder who has been bitten by the Bonneville bug that we call "salt fever." I ran into him out on the salt in 1999 and had a chance to get a few photographs at various times during the week. Every time I looked at the roadster, I liked it more. He sent some info on the car and I'll let it read as he sent it to me:

"Well, here's her stats: I'm running a 383 stroker, that I built. Machine work by Stirtz Machine in Oakland, Edelbrock RPM heads, Speed Demon carb, the tranny is a Richmond Super T-10, rear end is a Halibrand V-8, front brakes are now those new SoCal Speedshop Buick replicas, final drive gear ratio I believe is 3.48 to 1. Roy Brizio built the frame, and I assembled the whole car, and hand fabbed the roof. The hood and grille shell are real '32 Ford steel, the body is a Wescott, and the interior is by Sid Chavers. Bodywork and paint prep on frame and body I did, but it was sprayed by Marcos at Lucky 7 Customs in Antioch, California."

It's a hot rod, and he is not afraid of getting it dirty, which is somewhat evident in the photographs. The car is "flocked," Bonneville style, after driving out on the somewhat damp salt. The '32 was photographed in front of the Stateline Casino in Wendover, Nevada, or Utah, depending on which end of town you are parked in. The roadster is very comfortable for long drives, as Brett set the seat back, way back.

The second part of the story is that the car is now being built to run at Bonneville or the dry lakes as a full-on race car. This is what I meant by the comment about "salt fever" in the first paragraph. I saw some pictures of the car in progress. It looks good, and I'm looking forward to seeing it out there.

Right
Many believe that the 327-ci Chevy small-block to be one of the best that Chevy made. Paul Bos selected this version to put in his and Sallie's '28 Ford roadster pickup. It fits with the late 1950s–early 1960s time period, which is the style that he built the car to fit. He added an Engle cam to the engine for that nice lope, and just enough compression at 9.5:1 to give it a sharp tone. He then topped it off with a Z28 manifold and Edelbrock carburetor. The engine's hooked to a T-10 four-speed transmission and a '40 Ford rear end with a Halibrand quick-change center section. He then put the drivetrain in-between '32 Ford rails with Model A cross-members and springs and added a very traditional dropped and drilled I-beam axle front end. Paul had the '28 roadster pickup body lengthened 2 inches in the doors and rear quarters. He also shortened the bed and left on the original Model A grill shell. Jimmy Schoen and Jesse Elzalde painted it with flattened black acrylic enamel and then Dave Gade stitched up a 1950's-style black-and-white interior. Well-known artist and personal friend Bob McCoy added a few artistic touches to the '28, including the striping on the glossy black gas tank in the rear bed. The cowl had been reworked to fit the Pastech Duvall windshield, and Paul decided to run 16-inch Kelsey Hayes wire wheels, with the rears widened 2 inches. The roadster is perfect. Paul has been around hot rods all his life, and he knows what he likes. The rides in the garage belong to Bill Vinther, and it was at his place that I photographed Paul's roadster pickup.

Don Small's '32 Ford roadster has been well thought out and exe-cuted. This car is a great example of a mid- to late 1950s hot rod and the detail work is incredible. The 327-inch engine was built by Danny Brewer at Shaver Racing Engines to wind tight, and the sound coming through the 3-inch exhaust is indeed sweet. The transmission is a '92 Chevy truck overdrive five-speedwith a Model A floorshift lever. Dave Enmark set up the Halibrand V-8 quick-change with '36 bells and wishbones, and a set of 9-inch axles. The chassis started with a primo original frame, in which the front cross-member was raised 1 inch and the rear was replaced with a Model A cross-member to clear the quick-change. The frame has been boxed and strengthened to minimize any stress going to the body. A '40 Ford steering column mates to a Vega cross-steer-ing box and is topped off with a '40 deluxe wheel and one-off V-8 horn button. The front wheels are 4x16-inch '40 Fords with Denman 600x16 "big" whitewalls, and the rears are 16x6-inch with Firestone "really big" sugar donuts (wide whitewalls). The '47 Mercury caps complete the look. The fiberglass body has had the deck lid skinned in steel and louvered. The gauge panel is an NOS Philco accessory piece and the headlights are old Pepboys gener-ics. The taillights are original '50 Pontiacs, and the license plate light was made from a fender lip of a '51 Indian. The windshield was chopped 3-1/4 inches, and the seat was set back and raked for a very low driver and pas-senger profile. Don's roadster sits very cool from either the inside or outside. It looks like a hot rod, sounds like a hot rod, and it drives like a hot rod. Don especially thanks Bill Vinther for the many hours of valuable help and wonderful finish welding, as well as Cal Tanaka for making the body shape just right. Dave Gade in Corona stitched up the period-perfect black-and-white interior. This '32 was made to drive, and it gets driven. Don says it's his all-time favorite, and it is a regular on a well-known Southern California Reliability Run.

I first saw Dave Mathison's '35 Ford roadster in Colorado sometime in the mid-1980s. I photographed it then, and have found that every time I see it, I take a couple of shots. I finally ran into the car and Dave at the same time up in Washington in 1996, and it was then that I learned some of its history. It originally had a 1936 nose and front fenders, even though it was registered as a 1935, which it is. It was a *Hot Rod* magazine feature car in 1952, and Dave bought it in 1968. It was wrecked in 1969, and at that point, rebuilt with 1935 sheet metal. The top has been chopped 4-1/2 inches, and the white tucked and rolled interior has been matched up with a '40 Ford dash and steering wheel. When Dave purchased the car, it had a '50 Olds 303-inch engine in it. In 1977 he replaced it with a '68 Olds 350-inch engine. After 120,000 miles, that engine was replaced with the '66 Chevy 327-ci small-block that is in the car today. In 1996, Dave had logged 220,000 miles on the car. Just in case you think this car is just a quiet cruiser, I should mention that the 327-inch engine is running ported and polished 202 heads and 10:1 compression.

Tim and Arlene Stromberger's '32 roadster highboy was built for pure enjoyment. If you read the license plate, it says "IBUILDM," which Tim does in his Spokane area shop. He has put together many expensive rides, but wanted one that took them back to the pure enjoyment of traditional hot rodding. The '53 Mercury flathead is dressed with Edelbrock heads, a Weiand two-carb manifold, a Harmon-Collins dual coil distributor and Fenton headers. A Saginaw four-speed transmission carries the power back to the Halibrand V-8 quick-change. He used a Wescott body with the 3-inch rolled rear pan, chopped the windshield and top 2 inches and painted it with black Krylon. He said it took nine cans. The original old five-gallon Moon tank serves as a radiator overflow tank. Tim said that the project actually started from the set of 12-spoke Americans mounted on the front of the roadster, which had been hanging on the shop wall, looking for a home. Tim and Arlene put 5,000 miles on the car the first year with nary a problem.

Eric Perkin's '36 Ford roadster was almost put into the custom section just because of some of the subtle, but very effective body modifications. The running boards were narrowed by a previous owner long ago, and the fenders were reshaped where they meet with the narrowed boards. Eric made the original model of the bullnose and had it cast in solid bronze at a local foundry. He also chopped the top, cutting down the original top irons. This roadster is suspended with buggy springs, full wishbones, and a dropped axle in front, with '56 Ford pickup brakes and a later Ford rear end. The OHV V-8 Chevy small-block with Olds valve covers is followed by a three-speed overdrive transmission shifted with a '40 Ford column shift setup. The '49 Ford dash was narrowed and installed by the owner. Eric has owned the car since the late 1970s and said that the history of the car is a little sketchy at best. Whoever had the car before started a beautiful vision. The first time I saw the car was in 1991, out on the salt at Bonneville. The black lacquer paint showed the checks of age in 1992, and when I saw the car in 1999, it still had the same paint on it. These photographs were taken in 1992, at Bonneville, the year of the storm, or at least one of them.

Mickey Ellis used to own this Hilborn-injected, Chevy small-block–powered '32 Ford highboy pickup. He and Brent Bodily built the car for drag racing and ran it a few years before Mickey bought him out and ran it on the streets. The body has a 4-inch chop, it's set back on the frame 4 inches, and the cowl has been extended 4 inches, all to get some more weight back on the rear tires for drag racing. It is all hot rod right down to the chopped top, flames, Moon tank, roll bar, bias-ply wide whitewall tires, steel wheels, and that beautifully hand-formed and well-louvered bed. It was sitting on the road just above the salt at Bonneville in 1992 when I photographed it, and that is Don Palfreyman's flamed '47 Tudor sedan in the background. Mickey said he had to completely go through the engine after that year, as the injectors pulled salt down into the engine. Mickey is out there on the salt every year during Speedweek. Scott Hammon now owns the car, and it's back on the drag strip, with a little street time in the driving scenario.

Dave Tarvin's bright yellow '31 Model A coupe attracts attention wherever it goes. The bright color helps, but it is really the combination of everything gathered to put it together, and how it was put together, that keeps your attention. The balanced and tripowered 10.5:1 327-ci Chevy small-block is beautifully detailed. The chassis, built by Doug Maclanders, rides on a traditional buggy sprung, dropped and drilled I-beam front axle, and a triangulated four-bar and coil over rear suspension, tied to a Ford 9-inch rear. This '31 has the same wheelbase as a '32, which visually proportions everything better. Chop the body 3 inches, channel it 4 inches, recess the firewall, add hairpins, wide whitewall Firestones and steel wheels, then a white tucked and rolled interior with red piping by Phil Lowe, and you have a late 1950s period hot rod. Ted Hawkins replaced the floor and firewall, Ed Pearson massaged the body into prepaint readiness and Tim Kennedy sprayed the "lemon chrome yellow" PPG urethane paint all over it. Dave thanks Jack Williams and his wife, Debra, for making it all work out. I photographed the '31 at Puyallup and caught another 1950s style '32 as background.

I had a chance to photograph Jim Stroupe's '27 T roadster in 1999, out on the Bonneville salt flats, after he had driven the car out from the Bay Area. We had to wait a few days, because he was understandably reluctant to drive through the small "lake" to get out to the pits during Speedweek. It did finally dry off enough, and we were able to get this photograph. You can have no better setting for a very traditionally built hot rod. The salt was still a little damp, as you can see from the headers and the side of the roadster. The Brizio-built '27 has been put together following Jim's specs, from parts that he has collected through the years with this car in mind. It harkens back to earlier days, sitting on a nicely detailed '32 frame with many early and traditional features, such as buggy sprung axles front and rear, an early V-8 Halibrand quick-change, hairpins, steel wheels, and bias-ply wide whites. The body is stock steel with a '32 style dash and a chopped windshield. The Sic Chavers rolled and pleated off-white interior is accented with blue piping. The blue paint is a special mix, picked out by Jim, and painted by the Toy Works. The power comes from a well-worked-over Chevy 350 small-block accented by three deuces, headers, and all the correct brightwork. The transmission is a Muncie four-speed, so yes, the car has three pedals, and obviously, Bonneville being the distance it is from the Bay Area, it goes without saying that Jim drives it.

Right
Joe Davis picked up this '26 Model T Touring as a project in 1992. He got it running in 1997, and was towed home three times, after which he contacted Vern Tardel. Between Vern, his son Keith, and Kent Fuller, who did all the special sheet metal work on it, the car was finished. Kent mentioned that he had this car in his mind for 30 years. Some of the body modifications include rolled and louvered rocker panels, a chin spoiler, a three-piece aluminum hood with side louvers, and a 6-inch chopped and laid back windshield. The front seat was moved back 4 inches and down 2 inches for comfort. The Model A chassis was shortened and narrowed, and the '32 rear frame horns protrude through the rear of the tub with a spreader bar and '34 taillights mounted on '32 arms. The '35 Ford wire wheel centers were welded to VW rims in front and 7-inch Fords in back for the "big and little" wide white tire combination. The T touring was photographed out on the salt at Bonneville in 1999 during Speedweek.

71 The Traditional Hot Rod

Jim Lindsey's '56 Ford F100 is really a classic example of a traditional 1950s hot-rod truck. He uses it to tow his equally yellow nostalgic '24 hemi-powered altered T roadster. This F100 is the perfect mate to the altered, and it fits the 1950s–1960s drag support vehicle ambiance. Jim moved the front suspension and wheel wells forward 4 inches. It looks like it should have been that way on the originals and it's an improvement, especially as low as this one sits. Jim also kept the Y-block engine, a 312-ci Ford with a 3/4-race cam and three-deuce Stromberg carburetor setup on an Edelbrock manifold. The hood is louvered and the basically stock interior is finished off in rolled and pleated black Naugahyde. The F100 was photographed in Baker City, Oregon, and later out on the salt at Bonneville. Jim likes racing.

A group of us were hanging out one evening at the Pleasanton West Coast Nationals some time in the mid- to late 1990s. Actually I was photographing a group of traditional hot rods when Eddie Cole pulled into the group with this '32 roadster. It got our attention and was welcomed as a nice addition to the group. The six two-barrel carburetor setup is one of the first things that catch your eye, but in looking the roadster over, one continues to find plenty of authentic and additional hot-rod goodies, such as the gauges, hairpins, drilled front axle, and Buick drums. Bright red paint with an all white interior works, as does the chromed front and rear traditional buggy sprung suspension setups. The headers were homebuilt, and all frame work was done by Eddie, such as boxing, cross-members and motor mounts. He actually sold the roadster to Ted Perez as I was photographing it, and as far as I know, Ted still owns it.

BILL VINTHER'S '34 COUPE

Many of you might be familiar with Bill Vinther's "right-on" orange '34 Ford three-window hot rod. Bill started with a gutted '34 steel body and a swap meet frame before it reached the point you see now. It has graced many magazines and even Pat Ganahl's video, which I think now is collectible. It's an appropriate car for this section and it's all hot rod. Bill did all the work and fabrication required to bring it to the finished stage you see in the photographs. He is a consummate craftsman and has an eye for making things work visually as well as functionally. Bill's '34 gets driven, and believe me, it's a joy to ride in. I remember a drive through the bay area on the way up to Roy Brizio's shop in South San Francisco. It was Monday morning, and everybody else was on the way to work and we were cruising, just enjoying the morning. I saw a lot of envy on the faces of BMW and Mercedes drivers that morning.

Bill's '34 stands out visually; it has no extra frills built into it, i.e., no stereo, no air, or power anything; and it has a noisy "cackly" engine—a 327-ci Chevy—with enough compression (10.5:1) and cam (a lumpy Engle) that you hear it coming. The undercarriage, floor pan, and suspension are all as nicely detailed as the top. The headliner is nonexistent, but has some Cal Tanaka flames gracing the space. It is a perfect example of a late 1950s and early 1960s hot rod.

I asked Bill to add a few comments about the late 1950s and early 1960s era in traditional hot rodding, which he was gracious enough to take the time to do.

Traditional Hot Rods: it means different things to different rodders. Whether it's flatheads and wishbones, or small-block Chevys and hairpins, I like 'em all. But I have to admit, it's the late 1950s to mid-1960s kind of rods that blow my skirt up.

Why this particular era? Well first of all, probably more than any other time in rodding, it was this 8-to-10-year period that saw many old Fords lose their flatheads in favor of overhead V-8's (sorry Vern). But it's more than the proliferation of overheads.

Hot rodders wanted race car parts on their rides! And have you ever noticed how many race car parts ended up on bitchin,' Bad-O, traditional Hot Rods? Bell steering wheels, tachometers, Moon tanks, aluminum steering column drops, and gauge housings. What about quick-change rear ends, ladder bars, American five-spokes, Halibrands, E.T. IIIs, and dirt-track tires? All this stuff is part of the mix.

But what is it about cars like Dennis and Debbie Kyle's highboy roadster, or Cal Tanaka's '33 coupe that I find so "right"? Great aesthetics to be sure. Both the Kyles and Tanaka get an A-plus in that subject. But you know what else? Neither of the owners ordered a 1-(800)-BILLET part and glued it on their car, just because it was available by mail in two days. Nope. They searched swap meets and wrecking yards, or fabricated whatever they needed, so the cars would not end up "off track" aesthetically. Anything less is a recipe for a car with no soul, no direction.

How about the lumpy-cammed 10.5-to-1 motors that set off car alarms and rattle every window in the neighborhood? Yep, and don't forget the louvers, flames, Tommy the Greek and Von Dutch style striping, buggy springs, and dropped axles. And you won't find any fat 14-inch wheels and tires on the front either. No, we're talking 15x4s with 145s here.

Window moldings were meant to be chromed, and Buick finned brake drums were made to be polished. Windshield frames, door hinges and handles? Celebrate 'em, don't toss 'em!

But whatever you do, don't listen to the high-tech street rodders: BLACK PLEATED NAUGAHYDE WILL NOT HURT YOU, and is in no way responsible for my opinionated, primitive thinking.

After all, everyone knows it was the solid lifter noise that caused that.

I first ran into Dennis and Debbie Kyle at Bonneville in 1991. I spent some time talking to them and photographing their '32 Ford highboy roadster. It's a small world and I'll tell you a little story as to why and how it relates to Dennis and Debbie. I kept in touch with them and a year or so later, we talked about meeting at Pleasanton, or the West Coast Nationals in California. Dennis and Debbie said they were not going to make it, but that I should get in touch with Bill Vinther while there, which is almost impossible with that many people attending. I was covering the event for a magazine at the time and was wandering through the fairgrounds looking at the cars when I saw Paul Bos' '34 coupe parked in an out of the way area. I didn't know Paul at the time, but we got to talking about cars, styles, the distaste for power parking at events and such, and to make a long story just a little shorter, we decided to get together later for a short photo session and a bite to eat. After the shoot, Paul said he had talked to some other friends from the Southern California area about meeting for dinner also; they ended up being Bill Vinther, Cal Tanaka, and Don Small. I have the utmost respect for all these guys and find their creativity and hot-rod values paralleling my tastes. Dennis and Debbie Kyle were the original link, and their '32 roadster was the visual thing that pulled it together. I know this is not something usually written into a book, but all these people have become good friends, and I have learned a lot from them. They are at the core of the culture.

This roadster body and frame, which was raced at Bonneville in 1978 with a blown Ardun engine, came from Tom Senter, a legendary hot rodder, Bonneville racer, magazine writer, and Ardun authority. Dennis and Debbie created this version with their own vision in mind. The stance is a key part to the look, and the 5-1/2-inch dropped axle, held in place with traditional hairpins, helps, as does the big and little tire combination. The Halibrand V-8 quick-change rear end is supported via ladder bars and a transverse buggy spring setup. The louvers on the deck lid, gas tank, and hood have all been graced with Tommy the Greek–style pinstriping by Dennis Rickliff, as have some other selected areas. The roadster can also go through some subtle visual changes to alter its look. The commercial headlights are equipped with quick disconnects so the car can be run with or without them. The Moon tank on the front spreader bar is also removable, but the most dramatic change of character comes from the multiple selection of tire and wheel combinations that they have, ranging from steel wheels with Moon discs or '41 caps and rings, to Vaughn Real Wheels, to Mickey Thompson five-spokes. They have now added a Wimbledon White set of tall skinny big and little wheels and tires to the group, which creates another look for the roadster. The engine is a very streetable 283-cid Chevy small-block, and the transmission is a tried and true Muncie four-speed. Terry Hegman had a hand in building the headers and removable top, which gets used on the many longer trips that Dennis and Debbie take. The interior is classic hot rod with a traditional "roll" on the back of the seat, Stewart Warner gauges, and a three-spoke Bell steering wheel.

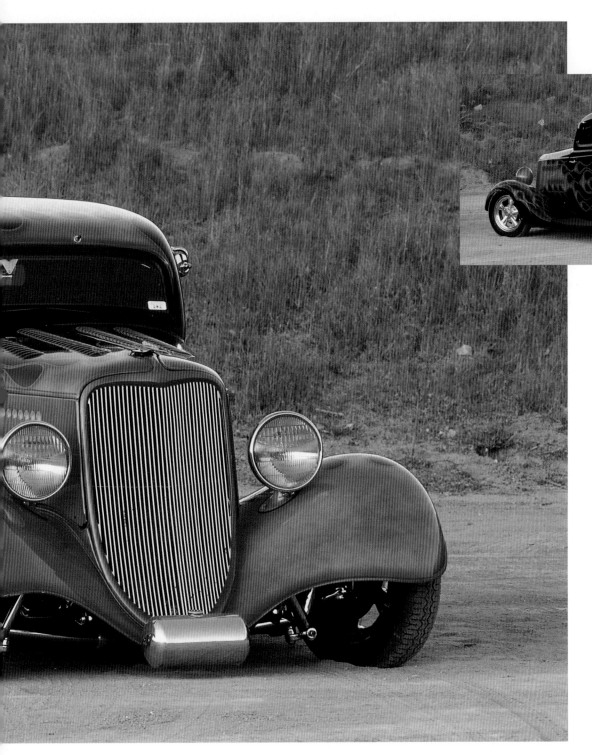

If I were to try and define what a full-fendered hot rod is going to look like in a pure visual and functional sense, this '33 coupe of Cal Tanaka's would definitely be one of the first choices. The stance and overall look of this car is, in plain terms, "nasty." The overcammed engine, the chopped top (4.25 inches in front and 3.5 inches rear), and the stance, which is as low as conceivably possible, are just the start of the visual feeling you get when you see the '33 coming down the road. Cal painted it black and added the flames, and if you ever had a chance to look under the car, which I don't see how you could, you would see that it is detailed with chrome, paint, and pin striping underneath also. The 355-inch Chevy engine runs a Velasco crank, Crower roller rockers, an Isky cam and valvetrain, 202 heads, and a gear drive. You hear it as well as see it when it's coming. In the cockpit, it is just functionality and good sounds, with absolutely no extra creature comforts added. This all-steel coupe gets driven often and the dinged peak of the front fenders under the grille attests to it. Cal quit trying to repair it. Bill Vinther crafted a piece to help, which fit over and under the peak, but it also bit the dust because the low coupe keeps coming in contact with the pavement. The Tanaka flames, louvers, real magnesium five-spoke Americans and knock-offs, and the general demeanor are all straightforward hot rod. Tanaka wouldn't have it any other way. This '33 helps define the terms "slammed" and "hammered," but . . . where do the surfboards go?

Left

Paul Bos is a consummate hot rodder and has been involved with the culture since he was a teenager. He built his first hot rod in 1955 at the age of 16, and he's been hooked ever since. All of his previous cars have been roadsters, so this '34 coupe is his first closed car, and it is a showcase for his taste in traditional and classic looks. Paul is quick to mention his good friend Bob Deburn; he says that without Bob's help, he probably would not have finished it. Another friend, Bob McCoy, a well-known automotive artist and hot rodder, applied the classic flames. I have ridden in a couple of reliability runs as "copilot" with Paul and I can say unequivocally that this coupe scoots and handles with the best of them. Looking out through the chopped windshield over the louvered and flamed hood is a prime view of the world, but not the best place to photograph from. The horsepower of a balanced and warmed-over Chevy 350 through a turbo 350 transmission on back to a '57 Ford 9-inch rear end provides the perfect combination for accelerated driving. The drilled and dropped front axle, finned Buick brake drums, hairpins, and a buggy spring holding it all together at the front, and the multitude of wheel and tire combinations that Bos has, all add to the traditional late 1950s, early 1960s look.

Mark Westrick got together with Bill Vinther to construct this hot rod orange '32 roadster highboy. Bill did most of the construction on Mark's roadster, which includes many of the features that you see on Bill's '34 coupe, such as the extensive use of louvers, right down to the little ones on the headlight buckets and the big ones on the rear deck lid and hood top. Mark built the '70 LT-1 Chevy small-block and added roller rockers and a Pete Jackson gear drive. The LT-1 engine was one of the hottest small-blocks that GM put out, conservatively rated at 375 horsepower. This roadster has the no-frills, basic, very traditional early 1960s hot-rod look, thanks in part to the polished Halibrands, skinny tires on the front, and the bigger and wider dirt-track tires on the rear. The Duvall windshield, the hairpin radius rods, classic black-and-white Moon gauges with chrome bezels, and the sprint car Bell-style steering wheel all add up to the right stuff. Bill's attention to detail on this '32 includes the stance as well as the construction and reliability for actually driving the car, hard.

Right
Terry Stoker's '32 three-window coupe was an old 1950s hot rod with no known history. Someone rebuilt it into a street rod in the 1980s, and Terry purchased it in 1995 and took it back to the 1950s–1960s again. The 5-inch top chop gives the coupe a "lakes" look, and the full fenders, a very low stance, whitewalls, steel wheels, and '50 Merc' hubcaps all help in the overall vintage look. The Chevy small-block–powered '32 was photographed at the Muroc Reunion in 1999.

Left top

Tom Schiffilea's '32 Ford three-window coupe is all hot rod. Tom says the car is the same way it appeared in the early 1960s except for the L88 big-block 427-ci Chevy, the 9-inch Ford rear end (which replaced a Corvette independent), the paint, and interior. It was previously owned and known at one period as the Doyle Gammel coupe, but it is all Tom's now. He made the car his. It sits lower in the front with a dropped I-beam axle, and the 9-inch Ford rear end is a better and more bullet-proof setup than the Corvette independent. The 427-ci Chevy, equipped with dual four-barrels and an Isky cam, hauls. Top it off with the killer purple paint, traditional flames, the white tucked and rolled interior, and you have a brand-new car. The original top chop is considered to be one of the best. The front posts were leaned slightly back, with 3-1/2 inches taken out of the front and 3 inches taken out of the rear.

Right

Ron Jolliffe is an Oldsmobile Rocket scientist, thoroughly into Olds power. He's raced them at Bonneville and Muroc, and he has powered this '32 highboy roadster with a 6-71 Mooneyham supercharged '49 Olds engine. It's the one he took out of the '49 Olds fastback that he raced on the salt. He replaced the '49 heads with larger valved and ported '56 units and put in an Engle cam. The '49 block was bored 1/8-inch to give it a displacement of 346-ci. Ron found the original steel body close to where he grew up in Texas, hauled it back to Hailey, Idaho, and when he could find time off from the race car and other projects, he finished it. Ron handcrafted many of the parts that went into finishing the roadster off, such as the headers and parts not as readily available for the Olds engine. A '57 Ford 9-inch rear end finishes up the drivetrain. He drives the car to his shop every day, weather permitting, as he lives in high snow country between Hailey and Sun Valley, Idaho.

Gene McKinney drove out to the 50th annual Bonneville Speedweek celebration in the '32 five-window, all the way from Tennessee. It cruises at 80 miles per hour without problems and gets 20–25 miles per gallon, which makes for long hauls between stops, as the car also has a 20-gallon gas tank. The top has a 3-1/2-inch top chop and the interior is race car–styled, with ribbed aluminum panels on the doors and kick panels, black vinyl, a 15-1/2-inch Bell steering wheel, and Stewart-Warner gauges. The Chevy 350 engine hooks into a Muncie four-speed and a Ford 9-inch rear end, which proves to be very reliable. The original boxed '32 frame is suspended at the front with a Super Bell 5-1/2-inch dropped axle, transverse spring and unsplit wishbone. The rear is suspended with a transverse spring and '36 Ford radius rods. Both ends use Armstrong lever-arm shock absorbers from a 1960s British car. Ford drums at both ends provide the stopping power, and the 15-inch steel wheels, 5-inch on the front and 8-inch on the back, are shod with radial rubber. This is the second time Gene has owned the car, which is another story in itself.

Craig Wallace originally ran this late 1950s–1960s style '34 Ford five-window coupe with a 6-71 blower on top of the built Chevy small-block. The car's best time at the drags was 10.90 at 126 miles per hour. The interior is caged and still set up for racing with a full harness and racing seats. The quick-change rear end, extensive use of louvers, hood sides, deck lid, top insert, and rear pan all add up to create a hot rod. Throw in the Firestone dirt trackers on 12x15-inch rear Americans, the 4x15-inch front-runners and "Limefire" styled headers coming out of the hood sides, and the coupe still looks like it belongs on the strip. Craig is now running a more "street" oriented engine without the supercharger, or at least he was until he sold the car. He has since built a '29 Model A two-door sedan that is a full-on racer, not the dual-purpose car his '34 was.

Below
Mike McClure's '39 Chevrolet coupe is an old late 1950s and early 1960s drag coupe. The radiused rear fender openings for racing slicks and the raised front end were part of the look of that era. Mike says he hasn't changed much on the car, just put a small-block Chevy in it and drove. It was photographed out on the Bonneville Salt Flats in 1997. I'm sure he spent some time cleaning it afterward, as it was a bit damp out there that year.

Ted Coons' '32 five-window coupe started its hot-rod life in Southern California, with the construction of the car in the hands of Don Small and Bill Vinther. The car then ended up in Steve Lemmons' hands for a few years before Ted got it. Ted had his eyes on the coupe for about four years, and finally all the planets lined up, and with a couple of cars changing hands, he took ownership. Ted then began massaging the car into final shape by color sanding some of the paint, changing the rumble seat into a trunk, and doing minor adjustments to make the car his. Part of the thing about real hot rods is that they get worked on. The owner is usually very aware of his or her car. It's part of the creed. The well-warmed Chevy 350-inch engine is connected to a Borg Warner T-10 four-speed and a Ford 9-inch limited-slip rear end. The dark blue paint is contrasted beautifully by the orange accents. The dropped I-beam, hairpins, and ladder bars holding the rear end in place all add to the equation of a very functional ride. The steel wheel-tire combination can be swapped to a set of five-spoke Americans to change the overall appearance. It is a relatively inexpensive way to change the visual direction and concept of a car, although vintage wheels now seem to be drawing a premium price.

Sam T.O.H.R.J. (The Original Hot Rod Junkie) is his moniker, and he and this '34 Ford five-window showed up at the 50th Bonneville Speedweek Anniversary in 1998, all the way from Strong, Maine. The car had just been finished in the 1980s, when it tangled with a tractor-trailer on the way to a rod run in New York. The car was totaled and the only thing saving the driver was the full roll cage and bulletproof frame, all built to Bonneville specs. The entire right side of the coupe was torn off. Sam and 38 of his friends (yeah, he said 38) rebuilt the car in a span of eight weekends, and since then he has added close to 50,000 miles to the car. The top is chopped 4 inches and the front of the body is channeled 4 inches. The grille, and what Sam thinks are '31 Lincoln headlights, draw a lot of attention. It also is only a guess, but Sam thinks the grille shell is off a Seagrave fire truck; he narrowed and shortened it to fit the hood lines. There are 616 louvers in the grille insert, trunk lid, and belly pan.

If you take an all-steel '32 Ford two-door sedan, chop it 3-1/2 inches, stuff in a 10:1 ported and polished, dual-four-barreled 392-ci Chrysler hemi, lower it, shoe it with big and little tires and steel wheels, and then paint it bright orange, do you have a hot rod? Well yes, especially if you put together all of this in a manner such as this. Dennis Bryden has an eye-catcher with this Tudor, and it does it stand out in a crowd. The stock frame rails are boxed and combined with TCI cross-members to create a strong foundation for the big Chrysler hemi engine. The transmission behind it is a 700R4. The front spring is a mono-leaf unit setup with a dropped and chromed I-beam axle and Bilstein shocks. The Ford 9-inch rear end is sprung with a set of coil overs. The front steel wheels are 14x6-inch and the rears are 16x10-inch which helps with the very aggressive stance. Al Swedberg did the top chop and louvered hood, while Terry Porch applied the bright orange PPG paint. The top insert was left in and the hinges and handles are still there. Add a Moon tank and hand pump to the front spreader bar, drop the stock headlights, and keep the chrome windshield frame, and you have a hot rod that harkens back to earlier eras. This '32 also sounds as good as it looks.

Pete Ingram came over from Australia in 1995 with this fenderless and much altered '32 Ford phaeton touring car. The steel body has been channeled 2-1/2 inches over the '32 frame and yes, the four-spoke Bell steering wheel is on the "other" side, made to Australian specs. The car took Pete 4-1/2 years to complete; when I photographed it, it was for sale and from what I heard, it did change hands. It came over on a six-week journey to the United States in a ship's container, along with a partially finished Ardun-powered steel '32 roadster. The motorcycle fenders were made from '36 Ford spare tire covers. For driving comfort, the front seat was moved back 6 inches and upholstered in rolled and pleated black-and-white leather. The headlights are off a '35 Plymouth; the top was chopped to match the DuVall windshield and has a full headliner. The car also has two floors with insulation in between for sound and heat control. Pete also wanted any pictorials dedicated to his late father Max, who helped with the car, but passed away just before it came over to the United States.

Bill and Tinker Lewis' '41 Ford sedan delivery is a classic example of the genre. The sedan delivery, which is sometimes is called a "three door," was originally built by Dave Marr around 1980, using parts from a '40 four-door sedan and a '41 sedan delivery. The right stance, polished American five-spoke Torque Thrust wheels, black lacquer paint, and beautiful traditional flames laid out and sprayed by Steve Simmons, all come together and bring about an enthusiastic response from the hot rod crowd. Add a hood punched full of louvers, with five on each side down on the lower rear hood sides, and you have a classic 1940 look. The delivery's stance is due to a Super Bell dropped axle and 14-inch wheels in front with Alden coil overs holding the '64 Chevy rear end and 15-inch rear wheels in place. The '41's drive train consists of a 350cid Chevy engine and a 350 tturbo transmission combination, which is a natural and easy fit in these cars. GM power steering helps the corners and the downtown parking, but those of you who know deliveries, know how it is to back into a parallel parking space with the rear visibility these cars have. Not easy. A Glide seat, covered with cranberry leather by Ron Lago, matches up with the Wilton carpeting, also installed by Lago. The bumper guards have been removed, and the taillights are classic '39 Ford. This car is a beautiful straight example of how good black lacquer can look.

Harold Aschenbrenner traded a Studebaker V-8-powered '40 Ford coupe for this '32 Ford Tudor sedan in 1957. The top was already chopped when the previous owner picked it up off a car lot, but its hot-rod beginnings are a mystery. Harold went through engines, trannies, and rear ends faster than he could count while doing what hot rodding was notorious for, street racing. This '32 Tudor has been through more engines and paint colors than most cars. The sedan has been seen in primer spots, cobalt blue, full primer, orange, red, Firethorne Mist, and finally black, which it is now. In 1975, Harold had the body dip-stripped between paint jobs and ended up having to replace most of the bottom part of the body, which was done by Al Swedberg. Larry Foss sprayed the black paint that is on the car now. The big-block Chevy was put in at the end of the 1970s. Harold mixes the tires and wheels from time to time to change the flavor, but the rest has stayed the same, other than the changeable grille insert. One of them is painted to match the steel wheels. Most of the time lately, Harold seems to run the American five-spokes. I have seen Harold pop the caps off (when he was running steel wheels) and take it for a couple of passes down the drag strip. The "street racer" is still inside, it's just that Harold, like many of us, has become wiser as to the proper time and place.

Pete Chapouris' '34 *California Kid* coupe was one of the reasons I started getting back into the hot-rod culture in the 1970s, when the television movie of the same name, with Martin Sheen, Vic Morrow, and a then-unknown Nick Nolte, came out. The hot was back in the culture, and between this car and Jim Jacob's '34 coupe, I began to see the visual excitement that pulled me into hot rods in the first place. Both cars became well-known icons and were perfect representations of the Pete and Jake's Hot Rod Parts business that they started. Robert Williams did the original piece of art that was the logo for the company, and you could tell that a new energy was coming, and an old traditional look was being revived. Pete's full-fendered '34 coupe was all hot rod with its chopped top, aggressive stance, louvers, and Halibrand wheels. The now-famous Manuel Reyes flames set a standard that is still considered classic. The price of chopped coupes almost doubled overnight. Now, of course, everything nostalgic or vintage has dramatically jumped in price. Pete is now at the helm of the new SoCal Speedshop and the *California Kid* '34 coupe is owned by Jerry Slover, who bought the original Pete and Jake's Hot Rod Parts some time ago.

Traditional and Classic Hot Rods from the Early 1970s Onward

The political and social change of the mid-1960s and early 1970s caused a major distraction from the hot rod culture. Many of us, because of the times, diverged away from the culture that we had grown up with. But some who did remain heavily involved in the hot rod culture saw a need for change and a redefining of direction. Hot rodding had veered away from its roots, and toward the "resto-rod" movement, crazy paint, and sometimes almost cartoonlike designs. This confusion, this lack of direction, was seen by many hot rodders as a demise of the culture. But there were those who still understood the importance and cultural relevance of the American hot rod. Among those who helped redefine and reintroduce the importance of the cultural core of hot rodding were Bud Bryan and Tom Medley at *Rod & Custom* magazine; the partnership between Pete Chapouris and Jim "Jake" Jacobs, and the personal cars they built; Jim Ewing and Gray Baskerville at *Hot Rod* and *Rod & Custom* magazines; Tom McMullen's *Street Rodder* magazine; and Tex Smith's overall involvement. There are many more who should be named in the effort to bring hot rodding back to the streets.

For me personally, it was seeing the TV movie *The California Kid* starring Martin Sheen, Nick Nolte, and Vic Morrow, and the Manuel Reyes–flamed '34 coupe of Pete Chapouris. The car was the star, and quite simply, it had the bad and nasty look that had been missing from the culture. The design was proportionally right, and everything fit. Between that '34 coupe and Jacobs' yellow Buick-powered '34 highboy coupe, which were on the cover of the November 1973 *Rod & Custom* magazine, the movement back toward traditional hot rodding was under way. These cars were hot rods in the purest sense. During this same period of time, the NSRA (National Street Rod Association) was formed, and strangely enough, it was probably also at this point in time, that the separation between "street rods" and "hot rods" started. Even the George Lucas film *American Graffiti* helped bring us back to the roots in its own way. Nonetheless, the energy had come back, and from that point on, the culture has thrived and grown into what we see today.

Jerry Slover has also purchased Jake's yellow '34 coupe to complete the pair. Most of us have come to associate these cars with each other, and they really did help bring the hot rod culture back to its roots. Real hot rods became acceptable again, inside the culture. Some of us rekindled old interests and passions because of these cars. If I were offered a choice between the two, I'm not sure I could make the decision. Jake's old '34 is all hot rod, from the front end to the back.

Mark Morton said this '29 roadster started life on the main floor of Oakland, with 4,000 miles on the clock, before the Brizio Family Award was conceived. But the roadster was inspired by a 1930s tether car built by the Rodzy Company, hence, the license plate that reads "Rodzy." The '29 Ford roadster body was massaged extensively around the cowl and dash to fit with the Hallock "V" windshield. The Steve Davis five-piece hood features '33-type side louvers, which work with the body lines coming down from the front of the cowl. Pete Eastwood did the chassis work, which is set up with a bulldog perch, Hollywood spring, and a Magnum 4-inch dropped axle in front, and coil overs on the rear holding the Ford 9-inch in place. It all works for a finely crafted and very low stance, which enhances the lines of the roadster. A Chevy HO 350 sits in front of a Doug Nash five-speed transmission, and Lincoln brakes all around provide the stopping power. The black paint is by John Carambia, who also is responsible for many of the custom-made brackets and the finishing touches on the project. The red tucked and rolled interior was upholstered by Whitey Morgan. A Lincoln dash panel holds the gauges and an old Moon column drop holds the steering column. Mark drives his cars, and believes that's what they are for, which, coincidentally, is also the philosophy of the yearly *Hop Up Annual*, of which he is the publisher and editor. We think he's right. The '29 photo session took place out on the dirt, at Edwards Air Force Base, during the 2000 Muroc Reunion.

Below
This roadster started its life on the frame and drivetrain that was in the Barakat/Eastwood two-door sedan drag racer, which was one of the only-primered cars ever to be featured on the cover of *Hot Rod* magazine, until very recently. It is all hot rod, in the purest sense. Joey drives the hell out of the car, and it's been broken and fixed more than once in its life.

Mickey Ellis has been around hot rods all his life, at least since his high school years in the 1950s, and he has built and owned many hot rods and customs. This '29 roadster pickup was actually built by Squeek Bell in Bakersfield for Tom Steele. Mickey liked what he saw and bought the car without test-driving it, but then he knows what to look for. All Mickey had to do was minor detail and finish work to get the car in its present form, which is clean, very drivable, and to the point. The engine is a Chevrolet 327-inch small-block running a Duntov 30/30 cam. The bright orange paint is all hot rod, and it works perfectly with the big and little tires on steel wheels. Everything in this car is laid out with careful thought and functionality, which is one of the reasons this car gets driven around 5,000 miles per year and has been seen all over the west. I ran into Mickey and the roadster at Bonneville, and, yes, it was out on the salt. The car was photographed at the Wendover airport.

Below
Gary Welter built this '32 Wescott-bodied roadster in 1978. He chopped it once and later decided to cut a little more out, bringing the top down a total of 6 inches. The folding original top was cut to match the windshield and is one of the striking features about the car. The beltline pinstripe was added in the mid-1990s by Herb Martinez. Little things like this can add just the right amount of emphasis. It's in the details. The secret is in knowing when to stop, which Gary did.

Mitch Allen wanted a hot rod, so he planned out this '31 Ford Brookville roadster body on '32 rails, and built it to his specs, which kept changing by degrees. He had Roy Brizio do the chassis work. Mitch then chose a balanced Chevy 454-inch big-block for plenty of power and torque. He followed it up with a Muncie four-speed and a 1957 Ford 9-inch rear end mounted with ladder bars and coil overs, to complete a solid reliable drivetrain. Mitch, and friend Chris Lovitt built the headers (which do uncork) and Andy Buffem took care of the finish welding as well as the roll bar and push bar, which doubles as a trailer hitch. Mitch chose a DuVall windshield and then commenced to build a folding top for it. The top is beautiful and it sits about 9 inches lower than a stock one. Chopped folding tops are difficult, especially when mating them up with the DuVall windshield. Mitch says that this was the most frustrating part of the build. Visually it was worth it. The steering column is race car style with a 3/4-inch shaft hung by a rod end under the dash and connected to a quick-release three-spoke Bell wheel. How's that for security? Just take the wheel with you, and nobody can drive it away. I've seen the car in three different colors of primer so far. I photographed it in red oxide. It is now Krylon flat black and sporting wide whites.

Left

Cliff Hansen's '33 Ford coupe is chopped and powered by a blown hemi; it's a hot rod I have admired for years. Cliff originally had Roy Brizio's shop in South San Francisco build the car with 18-inch 12-spoke wheels in front and 16-inch Halibrands in the rear. The semitubbed '33 has also been seen with steel wheels and wide whitewall tires, which completely change the look and feeling of the beautifully built and styled hot rod. The quick-change rear end finishes off the look from the back. I was at Pleasanton when this coupe debuted in the 1990s. The early hemi engine and the construction of the car is right on the money and very traditional in stature.

Harold and Martha Aschenbrenner's '32 Ford highboy roadster is a new car. I photographed it at sunset one evening during the 2000 Bonneville Speedweek event. Harold promised Martha the car in 1970, and decided it was time to get it finished. Harold is a long-time hot rodder and knew he wanted to build a hemi-powered '32 highboy. He actually had a Chevy big-block in the frame, but ran into the right hemi valve covers in a yard sale and changed it over to the '56 354-cid Chrysler engine, backed by a Chrysler four-speed tranny and a Ford 9-inch rear. The chopped top, American five-spoke wheels, and rolled and pleated dark red Masine vinyl help complete the look.

Grant Davis' tan primered, louvered, chopped, and full-fendered '34 Ford coupe is a hot rod. What you don't see under the hood is a B&M blown 502-ci big-block Chevy engine with dual Carter 750 AFB carburetors. Ed Monahan cut the 3 inches out of the top in 1956 when he was 16 years old. Grant picked the car up in 1992, with Dick Rodwell and Chris Boggess handling most of the bodywork during the build. The original '34 frame has been boxed, as it should be with that much horse-power, and a turbo 400 transmission transmits that power to a Ford 9-inch rear end with 2.47:1 gears. This car has to scoot down the highway with that ratio, and Grant did mention that he's had it well into the triple figures a few times. The car is driven daily and had 26,800 miles on it in 1995. Grant said it had never been on a "stretcher" yet.

CHAPTER TWO

The front view of Norm Benham's AA/FL tank gives you an idea of why these are so slippery in the air.

DRY LAKES RACING AND BONNEVILLE

Jim Lattin is now the owner of the original McAlister/Walker race car that ran at Bonneville in 1949, at the first SCTA meet, with Carl McAlister at the wheel. It's thought by some to be the car that made very first pass at Bonneville that year. To celebrate the 50th Anniversary of Speedweek, Jim brought the car to Bonneville to lead off the week of racing. It was the first car off the line on Saturday. This photograph was actually taken the following morning as dawn broke over the starting line.

O n April 29, 1899, Camille Jenatzy drove a wooden-wheeled, electric-motored "speedster" to a speed of 65.79 miles per hour, which made him the first recorded person to drive a car faster than 1 mile per minute. Louis Ross drove an aluminum-bodied steam-powered car to a speed of 94.5 miles per hour in 1905 on a Florida beach, only to be passed, a few days later, by a stripped Mercedes, which ran at an astounding 109.75 miles per hour. Model T speedsters were making appearances in the 1920s, due to Ford's very reasonable pricing and man's quest to constantly push the envelope of speed. With the advent of the Model A, what we could call pre–hot rods started appearing on the American automotive scene, especially in Southern California. The first organized dry lakes event took place at Muroc on March 25, 1931, which helped pull some of the racing off the streets of Southern California. It gave racers a place to "safely" race their stripped-down Model Ts, As, and other cars. Speeds of 100 miles per hour were commonplace, with 118 miles per hour reached by 1932.

The first and earliest dry lakes racing events were sponsored by the Gilmore Oil Company, which continued to sponsor the events over the next few years. Individual clubs from the Los Angeles area started taking over the organizational responsibilities during the mid-1930s. Clubs such as the Sidewinders, Throttlers, 90-mph Club of Los Angeles, Ramblers, Knight Riders, Tornados, Road Runners, Night Flyers, and Desert Goats were joined by the R.P.M. Club of San Francisco to help keep the racing events going for hot rodders, who mostly drove in from the Southern California regions. The Southern California Timing Association (SCTA), was formed as a nonprofit California corporation on November 29, 1937, and was originally proposed by the Sidewinders from Glendale and the Throttlers of Hollywood. The original founding clubs were the Knight Riders, Sidewinders, Throttlers, Idlers, Ramblers, Road Runners, and the 90 mph Club. Classes separating the stock-bodied cars from the hot rods were formed to allow more entries, which set up how the races would be run in 1938. At that time more clubs joined the SCTA, and by mid-1938, 23 car clubs were listed with 451 members. The new additions included the Ridgerunners, Dophins, Albata, Velociteers, Rattlers, Revs, Outriders, Pacemakers, Hot Irons, Mobilers, Night Flyers, and Mercuries, many of which are recognizable club names of today.

The last event run at Muroc Dry Lake was on May 15, 1938, when more than 300 racers showed up. The Army Air Force at Edwards Air Base laid claim to the lake bed, as it was within its boundaries and essentially disbanded the June event by showing up in force. Hot rodders were a bit resistant at first, but the soldiers returned armed, which softened the resistance of the commonsense hot rodders. They may have been stubborn, but they weren't stupid. The next 1938 event was held at the nearby and smaller Rosamond Dry Lake, with the two following ones being held at Harper Dry Lake.

SCTA-sanctioned dry lakes racing meets continued through 1941 at Harper Dry Lake, with speeds reaching into the 140 miles per hour range at the last meets. With the entrance of the United States into World War II, racing came to a standstill, not resuming with full sanctioned events until the war ended.

Post-World War II dry lakes racing in Southern California was part of a movement that saw the beginnings of hot rod culture entering the consciousness of American popular culture. Returning soldiers brought back an ingenuity that came from keeping the war machines running. They brought back a financial prosperity from back pay, which joined with the renewed economy that had blossomed throughout the country, particularly on the West Coast and especially Southern California. Traditional hot rods were born of this culture. The cars were stripped of anything that hindered the quest for speed. More horsepower was added with the advent of aftermarket speed equipment, which came from the ingenious minds of returning mechanics who had learned many tricks during the war, especially those associated with the air war and the effort of keeping high-performance planes running at their peaks. The supercharged P-38 Lightning and other planes, like the P-51 Mustang, were examples and personifications of high performance. The best engineering minds, coupled with the best materials available at the time, helped create a technology that naturally fueled the hot rod world. They worked with an ingenuity to make the cars go fast and to be durable enough to finish the race. The American hot rod was formalized with the World War II generation. Hot rodding wasn't something new to the time, but its explosive entrance into popular culture was.

Bonneville

Wally Parks, Robert Peterson, and Lee Ryan traveled to Salt Lake City in 1948 to start the proceedings that created the first official SCTA-sanctioned race on the Bonneville Salt Flats. The first SCTA speed trials took place August 22 to 27, 1949. Otto Crocker served as chief timer for the meet, and Bob Higbee was one of the names on the personnel list. Bozzy Willis, Ak Miller, SCTA President George Prusell, George Radnich, Doug Hartelt, Fred Woodward, Ernie McAfee, and Alex Xydias were all part of the original organizing committee. Dean Batchelor and Alex Xydias had the fastest car of the meet with a speed of 193.54 miles per hour in the So-Cal Streamliner. The two-way average was 189.745 miles per hour. The first car and driver is thought to have been Carl McAlister, driving the McAlister/Walker race car, which I had a chance to photograph in 1998 at the 50th anniversary of Speedweek.

I remember driving by the Bonneville Salt Flats when I was a young boy. In fact, the landscape from east of Wendover and Bonneville to Reno mystified me. There was a strange beauty to it, and yet a harshness. It wasn't a warm and fuzzy feeling. Later in life I grew to appreciate the expansiveness and the true beauty of the desert. The light is incredible. It is bright and crystal clear, especially in the higher elevations, which is probably why so many photographers love photographing there. Bonneville has all of that in a beautiful white minimalism, which goes through many changes during the day. There isn't a more beautiful place, especially for a hot rodder, than being out on the salt at sunrise. The air is still crisp, and the texture of the landscape is sharply defined with a light that is slowly shifting from cool to warm. The sound of a high-compression engine firing in the quiet of the early morning is incredibly awakening, and it belongs with the desert silence.

The other part of the day I find so incredibly beautiful is late in the day, just before, during, and especially immediately after sunset. I photograph almost to dark sometimes. The light is the best at that time, at least for me. There is a warmth to the tone, and the sky starts to turn colors that you sometimes don't realize are there until the film is processed.

The first day out on the salt flats every summer is a big adjustment day, physically. I'm usually excited about being there and look forward to seeing old friends; some I don't see but once a year, out on the salt at Bonneville. I forget that the brightness gets me, and as the day moves into its center and with the sun reflecting off the white salt surface, it takes awhile to adjust. Sunglasses are a must, and ones with complete UV protection are highly recommended. A type of snow blindness can happen out on the salt.

The next level of discomfort is the heat. One doesn't realize how quickly dehydration happens, but between the dry, high desert air and the heat, drinking plenty of water is another must. By the second day, I am usually acclimatized to the heat and my body has made whatever adjustments it needs to be comfortable. It usually involves a lot of sweating, which I don't notice so much because of the dry air. The third thing is sunburn. One doesn't feel it until the end of the day, but it is happening from all directions because of the reflective surface. I watched a veteran racer calmly, and politely, try to tell a young lady walking around the pits in a miniskirt about the reflective nature of the salt and where she might experience sunburn. I watched her reaction change from offense to what she thought at first was a crude comment, to one of realization that he was really just trying to save her from some pain later. I remember the first time I was out there, liberally applying sunscreen, but forgetting under my nose, chin, and ears. Those were the places that fried. I could feel them later that night.

I highly recommend picking up a Southern California Timing Association (SCTA) rules and records book to understand land speed racing and how it breaks down by racing classes, engine sizes, fuel types, and rules in general. It explains all that goes into figuring what class you would be racing in, what is allowed in the way of modifications, and what's required for safety, such as roll cages and fire suppression systems. It becomes quite involved, and I found it an interesting read, partially because I am hooked and would like to build a car to race at Bonneville, or on the dry lakes of Southern California, which would be El Mirage or Muroc.

What I have is called "salt fever." I'm not sure what it's called if one just wants to race on the dry lakes. There is a difference. The dry lakes can be incredibly dirty, especially if the wind picks up. The fine, gritty, alkali dust gets into every thing, especially cameras, but it seems to be noncorrosive. The grit will wear things down sooner or later, as it has done to my cameras, but I still wouldn't miss a trip to the lakes, and I feel a sense of history when I go there. The landscape is "right" for hot rods and race cars. It is appropriate and the dust kicked up by cars making a pass is a beautiful thing. If you have noticed, a large number of car companies photograph their product out there both in stills and film. The vision of a car running at speed, late in the day, kicking up a rooster tail of dust is quite enticing. Of course, to do so, one must be at a sanctioned meet and understand what it is like to drive that fast on a slippery surface, and you must be sure that the course has been cleared of any obstructions.

The Bonneville Salt Flats, on the other hand, seem cleaner, because of the lack of dust and dirt blowing around in the air, but it can be deceiving. It is a bed of pure salt. When it is dry, and I mean really dry, there can be a fine salt dust in the air that covers everything. It's not a significant problem unless it gets wet, and then it becomes corrosive and seeps into everything. I have noticed it on cameras so I am careful to keep them as clean as possible. The salt gets kicked up on high-speed passes on the course, and most racers and Bonneville veterans know how to deal with it and how important it is to keep it out of areas prone to corrosion. The worst time to be on the salt is when it is wet. When damp, the salt sticks to everything. We were out on the salt in 1992, when a storm blew in late Sunday afternoon, just as I was setting up a photographic session for a feature with Jerry Helwig and his '40 coupe. It came in fast, as storms can do on the desert, and lasted for about 30 minutes. Horizontal rain, and within that short period of time, the whole basin filled with 2 to 4 inches of water. We were in the pit area, which is located about 5 miles out on the salt. After the storm passed, it looked as if we were out on a lake. The sun broke through and as I looked around, I noticed tarps missing, people trying to find missing pieces to their pit areas, and last, but not least, portable toilets over on their sides. It dawned on me that it was a great opportunity to photograph. I talked to Jerry and we pushed his '40 coupe out of the pits and photographed it on "Lake" Bonneville, at sunset.

It was one of those opportunities that came out of a bad thing, which the storm was. It left a very wet course and shut down racing for about three days. What it did to my photography vehicle (a Camaro) is another story. The car was lowered, and just before I reached the pavement at the end of the salt I had to drive through about 10 inches of water, which the fan pulled up through the engine compartment and out through the hood louvers. We drove down to the one and only car wash in Wendover, and saw a mile-long line waiting to use it. We drove back to our room, had dinner, went to sleep and figured we would deal with it in the morning. Not smart. The line wasn't any shorter, and we were probably just recycling salt water at that point. My engine compartment was now salty white, and the starter was already giving me trouble. Even with all of that, I wouldn't have missed it for anything. The car can be fixed and cleaned, while the photographic opportunities only happen once, and I either get them or I don't.

Another Bonneville experience cemented my passion about being there. It was my chance to drive. Ron Jolliffe gave me the opportunity in his '49 Olds fastback, as my treat for crewing on his car, which my son, Nathan, was also doing. I had met Jolliffe at Bonneville in 1995 and photographed his Olds early one morning out on the salt. I found out he also lived in Idaho, and had a background similar to mine. I thank him for the experience and I have tried to put into words what it felt like. Most of all, I loved it, and was immediately hooked, which is what "salt fever" is about. I had to go through the rookie driver orientation, which involved testing my knowledge of the car and its safety features; it's basically a "what do you do if" session. I'm sitting in the Olds, fully fire suited, helmet on, and belts tightened, at which point I'm told to exit the car as if it were on fire. You have to decide whether or not the chute is needed, hit the kill switches and fire bottles (taking a deep breath before), stop the car, undo the harness, remove the window net, open the door and climb out over the cage structure. It took me 18 seconds, just 2 seconds under the limit of 20.

I'm sure a little heat, or real fire, would speed up my time, but I was reassured when I was told that it takes 20 seconds before one starts feeling pain in a fuel fire. Jolliffe said it only takes him 6 seconds to get out. We went over to the practice area to become more familiar with the shifter and everything else. Jolliffe explained the finer points and told me to watch the temp; not rev over 5,500, which was safely below the upper limit; and not to set off the fire bottles unless absolutely necessary, as they are $400 a pop to fill.

It's race morning, and I suit up for the first run, hand off my camera to my wife, Kim, and at that point completely stop thinking about anything photographic. I'm focused into making sure I don't screw up and, because of the short line, things start happening fast. I'm in the seat, putting on the head sock, helmet and neck collar. Then I'm getting strapped in, tightly. Bill Taylor, the starter, comes to check how tight and pulls everything even tighter. Between the harness and the wrist straps, I'm riveted down to the seat, making sure that I can reach all I need to. The fire bottles are armed and the car is started. I'm on my own and it's just a matter waiting for Bill to give the go-ahead. The push off goes without a hitch and I actually find low gear and pull away. So now it's watch the line, keep it straight, not too much power to keep from spinning the rear tires, watch the tach and shift at 5,500 into second, and the same thing to shift into high. All of this happens so fast that I feel like I'm just going through the motions before coming up on the one-mile flags, and by then there is no more shifting, so I just settle in, go straight, and try to build speed. My senses really come together with everything focused. For me, life really got clear at that moment, and there was a sense of adrenalized focus and a peaceful calm. You have such a gentle touch on the steering, and you are not conscious of anything other than the car, engine sound, tach, the course, and yourself. It feels right.

Up came the 2-mile flags and the quarter, at which point the timing starts with readings taken at the first quarter-mile and at the end of the mile, or third mile marker. Through the third mile, without trying to sound corny, it was spiritual, maybe mystical, but totally focused.

LAND SPEED RACING CLASSES

With the constant changing and upgrading of individual race cars, it is hard to print records, classes, engine sizes, drivers, or even owners, and be accurate, as they are constantly changing. Therefore, if I mention something that is out of date, or incorrect, chances are it was correct at the time of writing, or according to the latest printed records involving speeds, engine sizes, owners, drivers, classes, etc. I guess you could call this a disclaimer.

To better understand land speed racing, you should know how the class designations work. From this designation you can tell a car's engine size (within a range), whether it is blown or unblown, and whether they are running gas or fuel. It also designates what body style class the car is running in and how much modification is allowed.

Engine sizes:

AA = 501 cid and over	F = 123 cid through 183
A = 440 cid through 500	G = 93 cid through 122
B = 373 cid through 439	H = 62 cid through 92
C = 306 cid through 372	I = 46 cid through 61
D = 261 cid through 305	J = 31 cid through 45
E = 184 cid through 260	K = 30 cid and under

Vintage engines have their own special classes, which are as follows:

XF class—Any production Ford/Mercury passenger car V-8 flathead engine, 1932 through 1953, up to 325 cubic inches displacement.

XO class—Any overhead valve (OHV) and flathead inline and flathead V-8 (except Ford and Mercury) and V-12 engines, 1959 or earlier design, up to 325 ci displacement. Examples include Chevrolet, GMC, Hudson, Packard, Buick, Lincoln, and Cadillac. Foreign engines are not included.

XXF class—Same as XF class with overhead valve conversion heads, such as Ardun Ford flathead V-8s.

XXO class—Same as XO class with a specialty cylinder head, such as the Wayne 12-port heads used on Chevy or GMC sixes.

X class—Engines as described above, which are over 325 cid, but under 375 cid, shall be classified as either XXF or XXO. Specialty cylinder heads are not allowed in this category.

XX/PRO class—Limited to cylinder head port configuration as originally designed. This applies to the XXF and XXO engine classes.

Vintage Four (V4) class—Any pre-1935 American-made four-cylinder automotive production engine, up to 220 cid. Specialty heads are allowed.

There are some exceptions to these rules and if you are really interested, you can get a rule book from the SCTA (Southern California Timing Association).

These engine designations are always in front of the slash (/) in a car's class, as in A/, or XF/, etc.

As for body types, there are streamliners, lakesters, modified roadsters, roadsters, street roadsters, competition coupes and sedans, altered coupes, gas coupes and sedans, modified sports, modified pickup trucks, modified mid/mini pickup truck, production coupes and sedans, production supercharged, grand touring sport, production pickup truck, production mid/mini pickup truck, and various diesel truck categories which range from unlimited to diesel truck. None of this includes motorcycles, as they have classes all their own.

Some examples are:

A/BFCC — A size engine/blown fuel competition coupe	AA/BFS — AA size engine/blown fuel streamliner
B/GCC — B size engine/unblown gas competition coupe	AA/GS — AA size engine/unblown gas streamliner
C/BFMR — C size engine/blown fuel modified roadster	B/FL — B size engine/unblown fuel lakester
D/GMR — D size engine/unblown gas modified roadster	B/BGL — B size engine/blown gas lakester

And so on. Many of the cars shown in this chapter relate to these class designations. It helps to understand how these designations are made and what they mean.

I realized that I didn't have the pedal all the way down and went through the 3-mile flags at 5,300 rpm. The Olds handled beautifully, which says a lot about Jolliffe's craftsmanship and attention to detail. I backed off at the 3-mile flags and coasted to a stop. No need to pull the chute as there was plenty of runoff room. I gently turned off the course when the car slowed to a safe speed, and I shut everything down after stopping.

It was so quiet, and there was no one else out there. It was an enjoyable moment and I realized that I was drenched in sweat. I unbuckled the harness and disarmed the fire bottles, checked to make sure the electric engine fan was on and that the temp was OK and got out of the car. It felt so good to take off that fire suit top, and the gentle breeze started cooling me off. It was great, and I was hooked, big time, even though I wasn't sure how fast I had gone. The push car pulled up and my wife, Kim, asked if I wanted to know the speed then, or wait until I picked up my timing slip. I needed to know. It was 144.341 miles per hour average through the traps, a respectable run, but I knew I wanted to go faster. Beyond that, it was one of the most exciting experiences that I've ever had, and at the same time, one of the most calming and intensely focused ones I've experienced. It was close to a "spiritual" thing and very minimalistic at the same time. I was more worried about screwing up and embarrassing myself, or breaking something in Jolliffe's car, than anything else. The car tracked and handled perfectly.

I can only imagine what it is like to pass the 200-mile-per-hour mark, or to reach speeds above that. Someday, maybe I'll know. I have an immense amount of respect for those out there that do, and also have some knowledge as to why they feel the need and passion to do it. The people I have met in land speed racing are some of the best, and while there is a healthy competition, it usually doesn't override common courtesies. I have found that there is a camaraderie out there that speaks highly of the people involved. Parts, tools, advice, or even a helping hand will show up when needed. It is one of the last true amateur racing venues. People who race in the land speed events do so because of a passion for it. There are no prizes or big purses for the winners, but there is the respect and recognition of peers.

One other thing I should mention is that all records in land speed racing must be an average between two record runs. The first pass over the current record "qualifies" you for the record. If the second pass and the first average out to more than the current record, you get the record, and it's recorded. At Bonneville, these actually used to be run in opposite directions on the same course. Because of safety, and obvious logistical problems, the second run is now made first thing the next morning and the race cars are held in the impound area until this second pass.

This is a photograph of Bob Rufi, Bob Giovanine, and Chuck Spurgin, taken at El Mirage in 1948, courtesy of the Giovanine family and Bob Giovanine's scrapbook.

Running the four-cylinder Chevy at El Mirage in 1948 with, we believe, Bob Giovanine at the wheel. This photograph is also courtesy of the Giovanine family and Bob Giovanine's scrapbook.

Right
The S.C.T.A. 1948 top points trophy that was awarded to Bob Giovanie and Chuck Spurgin.

Bob and Curt Giovanine and the Number 557 roadster out on the salt at Bonneville in 1997, graciously taking some time to pose for photographs after a day of running the car.

Right top
Bob and Bill Pierson were the original owners of this '33 Ford coupe. The old Number 2D coupe has been restored by Bruce Meyer, who, I believe, bought the car from Tom Bryant in the early 1990s. Tom was still campaigning the coupe in 1991, as I saw the car run at Bonneville that year. Tom reached 221.898 miles per hour in the coupe, running a 304-ci Chevy small-block in the D/FCC class, with the D standing for engine size, F meaning fuel, and the CC meaning competition coupe.

An interesting point about the body regulations of the time, put together by the dry lakes sanctioning organizations, stated that the windshield height could be no smaller than 7 inches, but they didn't say anything about the angle. The coupe's windshield posts were laid back at about a 50-degree angle, which took an additional 9 inches out of the roof's height. The body was also channeled 3 inches over the frame. The coupe ran 153 miles per hour on the dry lake beds during the very early 1950s and was *the* car to beat at the time. The flathead run in the car during that time, built by Bobby Meeks, was a 267-ci with Edelbrock heads and a three-deuce manifold. The Pete Chapouris Group (PC^{3}g) restored the car to what you see today. It is a true piece of hot-rod history. This photograph was taken at Muroc during the first reunion, in 1996.

Right bottom
Bob Giovanine was on the cover of the March 1949 *Hot Rod* magazine as he and Chuck Spurgin, with the help of Bob Rufi and Duke Hallock, took the S.C.T.A top points honors in 1948. What makes this introduction interesting is that Bob, and his son Curt, got back into land speed racing in the 1990s with the same 1925 Chevy four-cylinder engine and a new roadster that bears a striking resemblance to the original. The engine, of course, has a few modern improvements, such as a billet head, built by Curt, and a full crankshaft girdle on the five-main crank. It is, however, the same 1925 182-ci Chevy block that Bob and his partners ran 123.655 miles per hour with in 1948. The new roadster, which is a '27-Speedway Track T, was built between 1991 and 1994 and first ran at El Mirage in 1994 with a speed of 133 miles per hour, and then at Bonneville with a speed of 138 miles per hour. The roadster was built around a tube frame with a coil-over rear suspension holding the Ford 9-inch rear end, and a traditional axle and cross-spring front suspension. A Borg Warner T-50 transmission is used, and Bob Rufi again helped by building the full belly pan and tonneau cover. In 1997, Bob and Curt ran 145.438 at Bonneville, setting a record in the V4/FMR (Vintage four-cylinder engine/fuel-modified roadster) class while they alternated driving chores. They then set a record in 1998 at the Bonneville 50th anniversary, at 152.202 miles per hour, with Bob driving the roadster with a 10 percent fuel mixture. We celebrated Bob's 80th birthday out on the salt, in the pits, while Curt and Bob were putting the car back together for another run. Sadly, Bob passed away the following winter. Both Bob and Curt are class acts; it is, and has been, my privilege and pleasure to know them both. Bob's passion for land speed racing was a big reason that the sport remains as it is today, a pure and passionate sport exists there because of what it means to so many.

The Jim Travis coupe was a regular fixture out on the salt of Bonneville, as well as the dry lakes, until it was sold in the late 1990s. Jim ran in the B/CC class for years with a small-block equipped with a crank-driven blower, and later switched to the VXF/CC class with a flathead. I always looked forward to seeing this coupe out on the salt and getting a chance to talk with Jim the few times that I did. Jim Travis has had a hand in restoring a few historic racing cars, such as Mickey Thompson's four-engine (blown Pontiacs) *Challenger* and the '57 Plymouth that Wally Parks ran at Daytona and Bonneville. This coupe is the old So-Cal Speed Shop coupe that was run in the early 1950s, and it is being restored back to that configuration. I'll miss seeing the Travis coupe out on the salt, but I am glad it is being restored, and will have to possibly start thinking of it as the So-Cal coupe. It was photographed at Bonneville in the mid- to late 1990s. The coupe is now owned by Don Orosco, and he is having Cotton Werksman build an Ardun engine for it. Don Orosco reproduced the Ardun heads, but only in an edition of 27 or 28 pairs. Alex Xydias owned the So-Cal coupe originally, when he was running the So-Cal Speed Shop, which first opened on March 3, 1946.

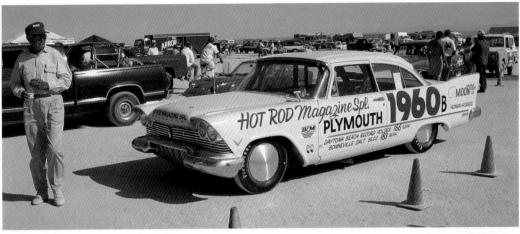

This Plymouth set a record at Daytona Beach at 166 miles per hour, and it ran at the Bonneville Salt Flats, reaching a speed of 183 miles per hour. This photograph of the car, which was built by Jim Travis, was taken at the first Muroc Reunion in 1996. Wally Parks, as well as being known for his long and deep important history in the hot-rod and racing culture, was instrumental in making the Muroc Reunion possible. He also was one of the few people there who had run at Muroc before it was closed by the military in 1941.

Left

The "Creel & Buck" '34 Ford five-window coupe runs a '34 Model B Ford engine with a Rutherford SOHC head. Roy Creel is the owner, and Sam Buck drives it in the V4/VGALT class. In the photograph, the coupe is in last-minute preparation for an early morning, or second pass record run, at Speedweek in the late 1990s.

Chuck Walbridge and Dan Walthen went to Bonneville for the first time in 1995. The both became so inflicted with "salt fever" that they decided to build a car to run at Speedweek. They took a '32 Ford five-window coupe and turned it into a three-window. They placed the body on a Lobeck-built frame and added a Ned Thompson–built 6-71 blown 392-ci hemi that runs on alcohol fuel. In 1999, five drivers qualified in the coupe for their 175-miles-per-hour licenses at Bonneville. Chuck and Dan then removed the Bonneville weight ballast, bolted on a pair of slicks and took it drag racing, and it reach a top speed of 158 miles per hour. They then converted the car to street trim and drove it to the Shades of the Past Event in Pigeon Forge, Tennessee. I photographed this car at the Bonneville Speedweek event in 1999.

The BMR (Berg, McAlister, Robinson) Racing '32 Ford coupe has been a regular fixture on the salt of Bonneville as well as the dry lakes of Southern California. They hold records in XO/BVGALT, XO/VGALT, XXO/BFALT, XO/BVFALT, XO/VGCC, XO/BVGCC, XO/VFCC, and XO/BVFCC, which sits at 195.282 miles per hour. They broke the much-modified 1952 GMC 322-ci engine pushing against the 200-mile-per-hour mark in the Number 285 XO/BVFALT coupe in 1999. This was an inline six, and you could see daylight through the side of the block. They will be back, and they are working on a new roadster project.

Mike Hegarty's '34 DeSoto Airflow coupe was built in 1988 by Dave Dozier and Ed and Mike Hegarty. They raced the car at Bonneville and El Mirage from 1989 through 1993, setting four records with one of them being 149.411 miles per hour in the XO/BVGC class, with a 323-cid Chrysler straight-eight and a B&M blower. Now, with the addition of Jerry Helwig's name on the car, they are running a 265-ci Ford flathead. The car was photographed at Bonneville in 2000 during Speedweek and at the Muroc Reunion earlier that summer.

Jerry Helwig's '40 Ford coupe was photographed right after the late Sunday afternoon storm at Bonneville in 1992. We were standing in 2 to 3 inches of water, the sun was setting, and the S.C.T.A course stewards were trying to get us to finish up so they could close down for the day. We didn't get back out on the salt until Wednesday afternoon. Most of the custom work on the coupe was done in the 1950s with the Boyd Brothers' names being linked to it. The history is a little vague. Jerry first ran the car at Bonneville in 1990, after driving it on the street. I remember seeing the car at the Goodguys' Pleasanton West Coast National Event around 1989 or 1990, with the hood up, showing the injected flathead. It stood out. The body modifications include a top chop, body sectioning with the fenders molded to the body, '37 DeSoto bumpers, and '41 Studebaker taillights. For Bonneville, Jerry was running a 270-ci early flathead, ported and relieved, Offenhauser heads, Arias pistons, a John DeLong ground cam, Belond headers, and a Kinsler fuel-injection system. The engine horsepower passed through a Doug Nash five-speed transmission before reaching the Halibrand V-8 quick-change rear end.

Ron Jolliffe renamed his shop "Rocket Science Engineering" because of this '49 Oldsmobile fastback project. He was originally going to build it as a street car until he visited Bonneville and became hooked. He reworked the car to comply with all the safety rules and stripped out the interior. He then reworked the suspension on the nice original car and added a 425-inch Olds big-block, which was bored to 432 inches. Ron ran in the B/GC (B size engine/gas coupe) class with the first outing in 1995. He originally wanted to build a roadster and was going to use this as a push car, but with the difficulty he was having in finding a steel '32 body, he decided to build the Olds instead. What he learned from running this car at Bonneville and Muroc proved to him that the car was not going to reach a record in the B/GC class. Because of the fastback design, the car had a tendency to lift in back, starting at around 160 miles per hour, which he was starting to reach with the current engine. It also was heavy and would require a lot more horsepower to push that amount of weight close to the record, which was around 215 miles per hour. Ron also ran a 1949 302-inch GMC six-cylinder engine in the Olds with a Vortech centrifugal blower in the XO/BGC class, but it had valvetrain problems. He had already started building a roadster, and with the cost and work required to run two cars, he retired the Olds after 1999. One thing about this car was that Ron had left all the trim on, including the hood ornament. He said it was just too beautiful to strip it off. I think this was one of the reasons the car was so popular out on the salt. It was the only one. I had a chance to drive the car once, which is another story, but it handled perfectly and felt great. Ron learned a lot with this Olds, and I know that it was hard to part with when he sold it. It will be back on the street though, with a blown big-block Chevy in it and in full race trim, just as it ran on the salt. It might, at some time, make a visit to the salt in the form of a push-car for Ron's new roadster project.

Terry Hunt took eight years to build this '53 Studebaker for Bonneville and dry-lakes racing. The car was in Phoenix, and Terry lived in Guam, hence the "Guam Realty" moniker on the car. He's an airline captain, so flying back and forth about four times a year to work on the car presented no problem. He credits his friend and NHRA racer Jim Hileman with a lot of the work and said he couldn't have done it without him. The main fabricator during the construction was Jim Moore. The first time Terry ran at Bonneville was in 1998, when the car was in original "desert patina" paint. It looked nasty, but if you looked close, the workmanship looked very impressive. They went 202 miles per hour and they have been back each year since. The car has since been painted and beautifully finished. I photographed the car in 1999 at Speedweek late one evening after a day of racing. Terry is running in the D/GALT class with a 301-ci Chevy Bow Tie block, a T-10 four-speed and a Franklin quick-change rear end. He is already talking about making some changes to the engine.

Left top

The "Geisler-Vail-Banks" '53 Studebaker has been coming to Bonneville for quite a while—the windshield stickers date at least back into the 1960s. Bruce Geisler and Gary Vail are listed as owners and drivers of the car, and they hold records in at least three classes with a 258-ci small-block Chevy, both blown and unblown, in fuel and gas classes. I should mention that many cars and crews at Bonneville and dry-lakes racing change engines and run fuel or gas to change classes, enabling them to hold records in more than one class.

Bottom left

The *Black Velvet* Studebaker, owned by Joe Gialich, is running a '69 355-ci Chevy in the C/FCC (C size engine/fuel competition coupe) class. Joe Gialich and Bill Sousammian are both listed as drivers, with Bill as the crew chief.

Bottom right

Jim Johnson owns and drives this '54 Studebaker five-window Starlight Commander, which runs a 1989 691 Donovan-ci 700 HC engine in the AA/GCC class. This photograph was taken in 1999 at the 1999 Bonneville Speedweek Event as they were preparing and waiting to make a pass. This is the old Jim Ewing Studebaker. At one time, Jim and Gray Baskerville (an editor for *Hot Rod* at the time) attempted to drive the car to a "land-speed" event, hit 200 miles per hour, and then drive it home. As I recall, the story said that driving that much engine, which, at the time was another high-performance big-block, was somewhat prohibitive for various reasons. But, even the attempt seemed interesting to me. That's hot rodding.

The Number 3738 Woody Parker '37 Willys Sedan is running a 302-ci Chevy small-block engine in the D/GALT class. This car went over on its top once and is now back and fully repaired.

Below
Vern Tardel and crew ran the *Salt n' Peppers* Nash at Bonneville for a couple of seasons in the mid 1990s. They added a 6-71 blower to the flathead engine and ran 147.210 for a record in the XF/BFCC class, which still holds as of this writing. Ed Bingelli is one of the crew and an expert in working a flathead engine out to its peak performance. I know that Mike McClure and Mike Bishop also had a hand in crewing on the car that year on the salt, plus probably some others who didn't get mentioned. The Nash has since been sold, and is now owned and run by George Carlson out of Oregon.

Below left
Al Turner and Ed Whitely run in A/MP and B/MP classes on the dry-lakes and at Bonneville with this Studebaker pickup. They hold records at both places with this truck. Al and Ed like the Studebaker moniker; they used to run a '53 Studebaker coupe, which also was a record holder for a time in the A/BGALT class at 221.238, only to have it passed by the Johnson Racing Camaro at an even 228.000 miles per hour in 1999.

Larry McKenzie and Keith Tardel's '27 T roadster ran for the first time at the 2000 Speedweek at Bonneville. It was really a shakedown trip to see how well the car performed and handled. Keith Tardel constructed a very solid race car and all indications are that it has a lot of potential as it handled and tracked beautifully on the salt. The blown flathead that they were running did just that—at around 150 miles per hour a rod let go and broke both sides of the engine block. Larry said that he hadn't reached full throttle and still had plenty of pedal left. They are working on a much stronger flathead that should handle the stress of running at Bonneville with a supercharger. These guys are all hot rodders in the purest sense, and many bring their late 1940s- and 1950s-styled hot rods out to the pit area to help. Besides Larry and Keith, a few others bring early-style cars, including Vern Tardel, Mike Bishop, Mike McClure, Phil Linhares and Ed Bingelli, "the flathead expert."

Left
Dick Flynn and Gary Harms are running a C/GR (C size engine/Gas roadster) or C/FR-(C size engine/fuel roadster) class '29–'32 roadster that is the old Number 360 Markley Brothers-Hoffman roadster. Gary's connection with the Markley Brothers goes back to the early 1950s when the Markleys were stationed at the air force base in Spokane, Washington, and Gary would give them rides back to the base, as hot rods were not allowed. Dick Flynn ran a '32 coupe at Bonneville in 1955 (to a speed of 162 miles per hour), and the Markleys borrowed Dick's hemi to use in their first Bonneville belly tanker. This car was built in 1979 and still holds a 210.341-miles-per-hour record in the E/FR class running a DeSoto hemi. That is part of the history. With the untimely passing of Bob Markley in 1997, it's nice to see the roadster back on the salt and out of retirement. Gary and Dick had already set everything up with Bob and Charlie before Bob's passing. They had already started fabricating all the parts required to run the Ford SOHC 427, which had been destroked to 371-ci. Dick is handling all the engine machine work. Gary has been responsible for getting the rest of it ready for the salt. The car always ran true and the construction was solid to begin with, so Gary mainly checked and freshened up everything. The Markleys required that three things remain intact: the original color, the original Number 360, and the hood and sides, which had been crafted by Harry Hoffman Sr.

Below
Ron Van Natta's '29 Ford roadster ran on a stretched '32 frame, with a dropped tube front axle with coil-overs and a rigid mounted Ford 9-inch rear end. What made this car different from the rest was the Ford 255-ci four-cam Indy engine. Joe Boghosian was the crew chief and engine expert, and the sound of this car, when fired, was incredible. Ron has since sold the car without engine to Rick Secord, who is now running it in the C/GR class.

Dana Wilson and Mike Waters are the owners of this highly competitive '29 Ford roadster running in various gas and fuel roadster classes, depending on engine size. Drivers are listed as Greg Waters, Dana Wilson, and Mike Waters. They hold records in B/FR, C/FR, B/GR, C/GR, and D/GR with a best speed of 230.569 miles per hour. This photograph is of Greg Waters getting ready to make a run in 2000 at Bonneville.

Greg and JoAnn Carlson's '29 Ford roadster runs various small-block Chevy engine sizes for different classes. It was built in 1993, and two sons have gotten their SCTA licenses in it. The engine listed was a 254-ci Chevy with Carlson injection and a Galbraith cam, with a Doug Nash five-speed and a Speedway quick-change rear end. The car has since been sold to Ralph Wisher in Montana, who came down to Speedweek 2000 to run the car for his first time in the E/GMR (E engine size/gas modified roadster) class.

Another roadster, this one owned and run by Bob Lindstrom in the D/BGR class, is a '32 body, with Ron Tasinski driving and Randy, Barbara, and Ryan Mead of Ravon Bodies crewing and helping sponsor the effort. Lindstrom's roadster blew an engine in 1999 at the quarter-mile at 189 miles per hour on a 190 record and came out the other end with an average of 186 miles per hour. They were back on the salt in 2000 with a new engine, and were trying to get the engine dialed in, adjusting the air/fuel mixtures.

The Marchese and Salter '29 roadster is out of Colorado with Bob Marchese and Butch Salter listed as owners and drivers. They also list Kenz & Leslie as sponsors, which is a historical name relating back to the first SCTA-sponsored Bonneville meet in 1949. The roadster is running a 304-ci Chevy engine, and holds the D/BGR record at 193.468 miles per hour. In this shot they are preparing the roadster to make a pass during Speedweek 2000 at Bonneville.

The Jones and Shadle Racing lakester used to run a 296-ci Mercury flathead. I photographed them taking off at one of the Muroc Reunion Events. Now I see that Ed Shadle is the owner and that they are running in the E/GL class, which means a different engine. Bud Jones is still part of the crew, but I guess he sold the car, or his interest in the car, to Ed. Things change and adjust at Bonneville and at the dry lakes.

Russ Meeks hand-hammered this beautiful '23 T body from .050 aluminum sheets; each panel is secured with the use of Dzus fasteners. This roadster is completely owner-built, right down to the D.O.M. 1-5/8x.188 wall tubing frame. No paint, just aluminum and tubing. I had a chance to photograph the car with half of the panels removed at Bonneville in 2000, which gives you an idea of the craftsmanship and thought that goes into building one of these cars. Russ is running a 270-ci GMC straight-six engine with a Super T-10 transmission and a 9-inch Ford floater rear end. In 1999 at the Speedweek event, Russ' son Cedric set a record of 136.090 in the XO/GMR class driving the Flat Trap Racing roadster. Russ and Cedric came back in 2000 with Russ' daughter Jacquie driving and broke Cedric's record. This is truly a family affair and a very interesting car. My question now is, when does Russ get to drive? I put two photographs together for this car as Russ pulled one side of the body panels off for a view of the internal structure. Russ has a beautiful sense of craft and an amazing ability to put it all together in an intricate, almost sculptural way. I thought you might enjoy a chance to see this view on the salt.

Above

Dennis Varni is the owner of the "stretched" Varni and Barnett P-38 belly tank lakester. Dennis is listed as the driver, with Cub Barnett listed as the crew chief. They are running a 355-ci Chevy small-block in the C/GL class, and it is considered one of the classics on the salt. The "tank" has history, as Bob and Charlie Markley originally built the car and ran it in 1959 with a 241-ci blown Dodge hemi, setting a 258-mile-per-hour record on alcohol, and actually hitting 280 miles per hour on a 25 percent fuel mixture. But this was only a one-way pass, so it didn't make it into the record book. At that time, it was the fastest open-wheel car. It originally had a 96-inch wheelbase, which Dennis has since stretched to around 130 inches. It is a beautiful car on the salt, and it is competitive today as wall as reminiscent of earlier times.

Norm Benham's stretched and rear-winged belly tank is running a 598-ci engine in the AA/FL (AA engine/fuel lakester) class. This photograph shows them at the starting line ready to make a pass.

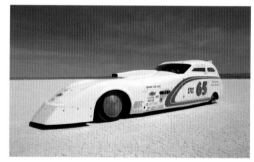

Earl Wooden's '47 Crosley two-door sedan has been a serious competitor in the unblown competition coupe gas and fuel classes for some time. He has been running B- and C-size engine classes over the years, with a best record of 278.350 in the B/FCC class. He has since switched into the AA class with a larger engine, and now holds a record of 292.288 in the AA/FCC class. This coupe always runs straight both on the salt of Bonneville and the dry lake beds of Southern California. I photographed the car at one of the Muroc Reunions.

Left top

The Seth Hammond lakester is considered by many to be one of the most beautiful cars on the salt. Tanis Hammond went to France with the car in the fall of 2000 for a special showing. This was shortly after she drove to a new 298-mile-per-hour record in one of the fuel lakester classes. The exit speed was above 300 miles per hour, and I photographed Tanis, Seth, the crew, and the lakester just after that record run. They hold records in about seven gas and fuel lakester classes, ranging from E-size engines to the larger B size, and they always seem to have everything well put together. The lakester runs very true on the course, which speaks highly of the construction. Seth, and the numerous drivers who have driven to records in this lakester, are fully enjoying the experience. Tim Rochlitzer originally built the car out of T-33 wing-tip tanks. The Seth Hammond lakester has been setting records since at least 1981, and the car is still performing and improving with higher speeds being reached.

Left bottom

Marlo Treit owns the Treit and Davenport lakester, and Ted Davenport is the driver. They hold a record of 329.431 miles per hour in the B/BFL class as well as records in the A/FL and B/FL classes. I talked with Treit at Speedweek 2000 and he mentioned that the lakester has gone as fast as it probably could, and then he let me see some photographs of the new streamliner that he is putting together. They have been running serious wind-tunnel tests on body mock-ups and are working out all the bumps that they can. This will be a car to watch for. This photograph is of the Treit and Davenport lakester at speed.

George Field's '37 Simca *Trackmaster* coupe was built in 1990 by George and David Casteel. The coupe started with a 392-ci Chrysler hemi, and was updated to a Keith Black engine in 1993. The Simca body is fiberglass and the nose section is formed out of aluminum. George set the A/BFCC record in 1995 at 300.509 miles per hour, but at the finish of the record-setting run, the car left the ground as it went through the traps. George's first words after everything had stopped and he was out of the car were, "Did we get the record?" As of the year 2000, the record still holds, as well as records in A/FCC at 264.667 miles per hour, B/BGCC at 231.285 miles per hour, and David Casteel holds a record in the A/BGCC at 258.378 miles per hour. George had the car leave the ground one other time, and has since redesigned the front end to what you see in the photographs, which were taken in 1999 and 2000. The original had uncovered front wheels, and now they are getting too much downforce on the front end. George was trying to work out the spring rate needed to keep the car from tearing up the front tires. The color photograph was taken just after sunset out on the salt in 2000, and the black and white photograph was taken in 1999, just as they were pushing off the starting line.

Tom Bryant's *Tom Thumb Special* is a '34 Ford coupe with a 304-ci Chevy small-block running in the D/FCC class. Bryant has been a competitor for some time, previously owning the original Pierson Brothers coupe and holding a couple of records in D/GCC and D/FCC at different times. Currently he holds the D/FCC record at 234.393 miles per hour. I should note that these records are constantly changing, so by the time this is in print, things could be different.

No information on this streamliner, which is new. This photograph was taken at Speedweek in 1999 just before a run.

I had the opportunity to meet and talk with Joaquin Arnett, the original "Bean Bandit," at Bonneville Speedweek in 2000. He is an enjoyable and gracious man to spend time with and he has a long and deep history with the hot-rod, custom-car, and racing culture, which involves all aspects of what this book is about. Joaquin's mother forged his birth certificate when he was 14 so he could get a driver's license, enabling him to take her and some neighbors to work. He actually started driving at an even younger age, probably around 9 or 10. Joaquin started building hot rods when he was around 11 years old, before World War II. The Bean Bandits Car Club was organized in 1950 by a group of guys who had gone to San Diego High School together. They were known as the Mexican Club, but really were a mixture of mixed nationalities, as they still are today. They competed at drag strips all over California in the early 1950s and ran a car at Bonneville in 1952. In 1953, Joaquin won the first National Hot Rod Association Drag Race Championship at Pomona. In February of that year, Joaquin was on the cover of *Hot Rod* magazine and the club was becoming quite well known. The club disbanded in 1960 because of families and finances and was resurrected in 1988. In the mid-1990s, the club had 41 members, of which one-fourth are original members. In 1989, Joaquin and his two sons, Sonny and Jeff, built a streamliner, powered by an injected Ardun-headed flathead engine. They ran this car at El Mirage in 1991 for a new record of 202 miles per hour in the XX/FS class. Joaquin, and his son Jeff, are fuel-mixing wizards. They have learned a method of mixing large percentages of nitromethane without blowing up their engines. Joaquin and his sons built a second streamliner with a 488-ci fuel-injected Chrysler, powering it to a class record of 231.946 miles per hour in the fall of 1992. The streamliner kept pushing the speeds higher with Sonny Barnett at the wheel. In May 1995, after making a pass at 317 miles per hour at El Mirage, the streamliner got sideways and rolled in a terrible accident, taking Sonny Barnett's life.

Joaquin and the Bean Bandits showed up at Speedweek 2000 with a flathead-powered streamliner, but they were running into a few problems. I don't believe they ran, but they held their well-known barbecue, which is always looked forward to by many of the Bonneville regulars.

Joaquin's history with the culture is a long and rich one that involves everything from drag racing in the 1950s, to land speed racing through today, and top chops and customizing as early as the late 1930s. Joaquin says he cut his first top in 1939. He has worked with many people and is a legend in the hot-rod and racing culture. He and the Bean Bandits, are, and have been, a driving force in the San Diego area and I wish I had the time and space to gather all of the stories. I do know he worked with Ed and Bob (Joaquin calls him Bobby) Stewart in chopping the Stewart '32 Victoria. He says he handed Bobby the hacksaws, marked where to cut, and told him to holler when he had finished. Joaquin then commenced to put it all back together with torch, dolly, and hammer. A few hours' work for the master.

In 1994, at the 2nd "Hot Rod Reunion," Joaquin Arnett was presented a Lifetime Achievement Award for his contributions to the sport of drag racing. He has received many other awards in recognition to the culture, including being inducted into the Garlits' Drag Racing Hall of Fame that same year. The Don Garlits' Drag Racing Museum houses a Bean Bandit roadster and the NHRA Motorsports Museum at Pomona include a rebuilt version of the Bean Bandit fuel dragster that won the first NHRA sanctioned race at Pomona. It was a pleasure meeting Joaquin at Bonneville. If you ever have a chance, ask him about the time he welded a silver dollar into a hole on top of one of his racing pistons out on the salt of Bonneville. As I mentioned earlier, the stories and legends go on and on and on . . . and they are worth listening to.

This photograph of the flathead-powered streamliner and the Bean Bandit crew was taken at Bonneville during Speedweek 2000.

Left bottom
The Larsen-Cummins streamliner is owned and driven by Fred Larsen and sponsored by Mooneyes of Japan and Mooneyes of U.S.A., Inc. They hold the record in F/BFS with a speed of 307.977 miles per hour as well as a record in the G/BFS class with a speed of 246.026 miles per hour.

The streamliner *Danny Boy*, which comes out of the apple country of Washington State, is owned and driven by Ed Tradup and Richard Thomason. They hold a record of 322.921 in the C/FS class. The photograph is of Ed Tradup and the streamliner, after making a pass at Bonneville in 1998. Jim Socci is the crew chief on this competitive streamliner.

Roy Fjastad owns and runs the "Fjastad-Maris-Kinne-Wood" '26 roadster, which runs a 360-ci Rodeck small-block Chevy in the C/GMR class, in which it is the current record holder at 224.874 miles per hour. They also hold a record in the A/GMR class with a speed of 234.276. The second car in the photograph is the "Fjastadt-Olson-Maris" A/ gas streamliner (A/GS), which is working toward a 332-mile-per-hour-record held by the Vesco-Nish streamliner. Both of Roy's race cars are sponsored by Full-Bore Race Products. Both race cars are extremely well presented and designed.

The Nish Motorsports 1957 John Vesco streamliner is a regular and a multiple-record holder at Bonneville, with records in numerous gas- and fuel-class engine sizes with speeds above the 300-mile-per-hour range. The Vesco/Nish car has a long history at Bonneville.

Right
Al Teague and the *76 Special* streamliner making a pass in the high 300-mile-per-hour range on the long course at Bonneville.

Al Teague is one of the true gentlemen of Bonneville. He is a serious competitor and always seems to have time to talk to people on the salt. This is something that I can't speak highly enough of for many out there. They are there to race, and have their hands full with that alone, but many will take the time to answer questions. I enjoyed meeting Al and appreciate the time he took at the end of a run in 2000 to allow me a chance to get some photographs. The sound of the Number 76 Teague, Welch, and Banks streamliner making a pass is so recognizable and beautiful, that it is hard to describe in words. You can hear it from anywhere out on the salt. This blown top-fuel engine has its own sound. I remember the 432-mile-per-hour pass in 1991 and the multiple records in classes ranging from "C" engine sizes up to "AA," which attest to the competitiveness of the car. This is the fastest single-engine V-8-powered car. It was the fastest wheel-driven car until Don Vesco bumped the record up with his gas turbine-powered 3,750-horsepower *Turbinator* streamliner in 1999 with a record speed of 427.832 miles per hour in the T/III special construction class. Al's previous "fastest wheel-driven" record of 409.986, held since 1991 and is, in fact, still the record for the A/BFS class.

I got this photograph of the Burkland streamliner just after it pulled off course during a pass in 1998. The AA/BFS streamliner is running a pair of 450-ci blown Donovan Chrysler engines, hooked up to a four-wheel-drive setup. It is owned by Tom, Betty, and Gene Burkland and driven by Tom. At the World Finals 2000 Event at Bonneville, they made a pass at above 450 miles per hour, but lost both chutes at the end, went too far on the course, and had to be dug out. I am looking forward to seeing this car run again, as it looks like the team have some of the performance kinks worked out. Now, if they can figure out a safe way to stop it, they will be in business.

A FIRST TRIP TO BONNEVILLE

Jay Fitzhugh went to Bonneville for the first time in 1998 for the 50th anniversary of Speedweek. Jay has written some in-depth articles for Steve Coonan and *The Rodder's Journal*, a quarterly periodical that many of us have a high regard for. It is a publication that usually sits on the bookshelf, rather than the magazine rack. After going to Bonneville, Jay wrote the following comments about his first time on the salt, and the post-trip feelings. I enjoyed what he wrote, as I hope you do, and I do still remember my first trip to Bonneville and the feelings that I brought home with me. The excitement has never truly left, and I look forward to each trip, every year. It truly is a photographic and racing paradise, at least for me.

The First Time

For years, magazine coverage of Bonneville tantalized my adolescent imagination. As an adult, I finally had the opportunity to satisfy a decades old yearning and participate in the 50th Speedweek. Nothing I had ever read or seen prepared me for the experience. Expectations and anticipation are usually dampened by reality; not so on this road trip.

The first drive onto the salt was surreal. I was in an Ansel Adams photo. The gleaming white salt against the dark mountains, with beams of light streaking down through the clouds, the curvature of the earth revealed. A 360-degree panorama that film can only myopically capture. All perception of space and distance were lost. Only after driving to the pits for 10 minutes at 60 miles per hour did the immensity begin to be realized.

Before the start of time trials, the pits were a magical place. Everyone was making his or her nomadic home. Not being a true racer, I was surprised at the amount of effort under way before any tires had rolled. With a year to get ready, why not come prepared? My experienced guide and partner, Peter Bennett, summed it up succinctly, "That's racing." While salivating over all the hardware, I almost missed the true story. The reestablishment of long enduring friendships, just like a high school reunion, sidelined even the most devoted mechanics and drivers from their preparatory duties. Bill Burke, a 50-year salt veteran, summed it up in a Will Roger's–like statement: "Some people think this is about cars or speed, but they're wrong. It's about people."

After the first dozen passes, the day settled into an almost nonchalant horsepower parade. Activities and conversations were interrupted for just a moment to catch a glimpse of the latest car to challenge the record book. Over the car radio, the SCTA announcer doled out the vital information. Just when I began to recede from the initial adrenaline rush, an unfamiliar, deep, earthy sound caused my head to instinctively swivel. Everyone with and around me had the identically timed reaction. Words ended in midsyllable. All eyes followed as the missile of the moment streaked past our vantage point. Even from the safe spectator distance, you could feel this guy go by. His stampede down the salt made the ground shake.

By midafternoon the first day, I was forced to remember that, for all intents and purposes, you're standing on a mirror in the desert. This is the most corrosive and inhospitable place on the face of the earth. Body parts unprepared for exposure quickly convinced me to cover up. (Be sure to wear your Jockeys if you're wearing shorts.) Long pants, long sleeves, a wide-brimmed hat and a damp towel around the neck made the week bearable. Drink a lot. At 14 percent humidity, fluid is being sucked from your body.

Nightfall brought forth a number of traditions, from the campers and roadside parties, to the hotel parking profilers, plus the late night efforts under parking lot lights to prepare for another day of racing. Most participants were sleep deprived in order to see the sun rise on the salt and the start of the return record runs in the cool morning air.

It took at least a week back in surroundings with grass and trees before my senses returned to normal. Sun overexposure was waning. I had time to catch up on my sleep. The sound, more than anything else, lingered. The singing of 8,000 rpm reverberated from an electric desk fan, or from the droning of the neighbor's lawn mower. Unconsciously, I strained to hear the next up-shift or the tell-tale sound of a spin, until realizing that I was no longer on the salt, and it was not an 800-horsepower motor at all. Speed intoxication, and now the hangover.

—Jay G. Fitzhugh

Drag Racing

Drag racing actually started with rolling starts on the dry lakes. Cars would be rolling at a slow speed, sometimes as many as five abreast and at some point they would all accelerate toward a designated finish line on the dry lake. While this is not what you think of when you consider today's organized events, or even drag racing during the 1950s and 1960s, it was a beginning. From these races out on the lakes, to the "street races" that were taking place on paved roads and highways, it was acknowledged by many involved that things had to be made safer. They had to find places to race that were not endangering the public, or themselves for that matter, and the best places seemed to be the many abandoned airports left over from World War II. It also got the police off the racers' backs, as the police were starting to clamp down on the street racing.

One of the first drag-racing venues was the Goleta Airport, close to Santa Barbara, California, which used to be a Marine base during World War II. The Santa Barbara Acceleration Association (SBAA) organized the events in 1949, but this was a somewhat loose, unorganized event. The first organized drag strip was at the Santa Ana Airport in 1950. This was later called the Orange County Airport, and is now known as John Wayne International Airport. C. J. Hart, Frank Stilwell, and Creighton Hunter organized the meet. As these drag strips and events became more popular, more started being organized throughout California and up into Oregon and Washington. Within a few years, drags had spread throughout the country and over to the East Coast. The sophistication of the cars increased, and builders reoriented the cars from the dry lakes racing venue to the drag strip. The cars had different needs and a much shorter time and course in which to build up speed. Standards were set at a quarter-mile from a standing start, with the first one to the end winning.

It sounds simple, but suddenly the cars were dealing with traction problems and how to get all the horsepower to the strip without just spinning the tires. The more the traction was improved, the more the drivetrain parts would break. These factors seesawed back and forth as the sport became more and more sophisticated. The dry lakes and Bonneville land speed racing events continued to happen with their own following, but drag racing was much more localized, with abandoned air strips across the country being brought into use by local hot rodders. The races could be held once a month, or even more often, while Bonneville and the dry lakes happened only a few times each year. The popularity of drag racing surged, and by the end of the 1950s, and into the 1960s the sport started to reach the broader public arena. Today it is big business and with many, it has become too costly to effectively compete on an amateur level. Possibly as a result, the nostalgic drag-racing movement has become popular with amateur racers, and these meets are held throughout the country.

The cars represented in this section relate to "gasser wars" of the late 1950s and into the 1960s. My brief involvement in drag racing was during the early 1960s, and my memories are of these cars. This was all-out racing in a sense that the first one down to the end of the track won. The classes were set up according to engine size and body type, and it was an era, for many, that was the height of drag racing. The racing was still reachable by average hot rodders, many of whom built "gasser"-style cars. These cars were essentially hot rods that were built just for racing, with some actually doubling as transportation.

High-octane gas was still available, so 12.5 to 1 compression ratios were still within the realm of "street driving reality." It doesn't mean that these cars were practical, but they were drivable.

The Mooneyham & Sharp '34 coupe and the Stone/Woods/Cook Willys were probably two of the best-known "gassers" of this era. The local strips catered to these cars, and the crowds loved them. Many aspiring drag racers would build cars of this genre, and while the cars cost a fair amount of money, they were still reachable and competitive to the average, but dedicated, racer. Toward the end of the 1960s, innovation in pursuit of higher and higher speeds increased the costs to a point that without a lucrative sponsorship, racers couldn't remain competitive. Most of the cars in this section relate to this earlier period in drag racing, with some being recently built for current nostalgic racing. Again, as higher and higher speeds are reached, the cost is going up, even in the nostalgic venue. I for one, miss the gasser era of the late 1950s and 1960s. Bracket racing has its place, and probably allows more people to compete, but it also homogenized the racing with its "break-out" rules.

The cars in the following photographs all belong to the past and present form of traditional drag racing, where the first one through the quarter-mile wins. Some of these cars could fit in the traditional hot rod chapter, and one in particular did, Bob Lick's yellow '40 Ford coupe, which he races in nostalgic meets throughout the West. This isn't for financial gain, but for the passion of racing, which is the purest reason and one of the reasons land speed racing is attracting such a renewed interest.

Front-engine dragsters that ran during this era were always a step above reachable levels for the average hot rodder, especially if you entered into the realm of fuel burners. I knew quite a few racers who ran unblown front-engine dragsters on gas, which was an affordable arena, but these were mainly on local strips, and even then if you started thinking about national competition, it became prohibitively expensive for the average hot rodder.

The Mooneyham & Sharp '34, the Stone/Woods/Cook Willys, the "Big John" Mazmanian Willys, and the K.S. Pitman Willys were as well known in the drag racing and hot rod culture, as were the big names in front-engine fuel-burning dragsters, such as Don Garlits' *Swamp Rat*; the Greer-Black-Prudhomme dragster, with Don "The Snake" Prudhomme driving; Connie Kalitta and the *Bounty Hunter* dragster; the *Vagabond* dragster; the Kuhl & Olson dragster; the Albertson Olds dragster; Art Chrisman and the *Hustler 1* dragster; Chris "The Golden Greek" Karamesines; the Howard Cam Special; or Tommy Ivo with his many creations, including the multiple-engine dragsters. Other names that come to mind are the chassis builders—Kent Fuller, whose name keeps coming up, as more and more of the cars are found and brought back; Jim Nelson and Dode Martin of Dragmaster fame; and Don Long and Woody Gilmore, who are remembered for their chassis construction. This was the time that sticks in my memory, and it was the type of drag racing that was heads-up and to the max.

Jim Lindsey's nostalgic altered-styled '24 Ford Model T harkens back to earlier times. He spent two years designing and crafting the car in his farm shop. It was built to be reminiscent of the altereds that ran on drag strips across the country in the 1950s. What you see in the photograph is a '53 Dodge Red Ram 241-ci hemi that has been bored .030 over. The engine is running a Chris Neilson cam, stock rockers, adjustable pushrods, shot-peened stock rods with Ross pistons, a Joe Hunt magneto, and a Weiand manifold with four alcohol-fed Stromberg 97 carburetors. Bob Lick, another Oregon hot rodder, crafted the zoomie headers. Alcohol fuel is used to keep the engine cool, making a radiator unnecessary—the water in the engine block is enough. Bill Carlyle handled all of the machine work on the engine, and the Powerglide transmission was reworked and set up by Fuller Automotive in LaGrande, Oregon. The Ford 9-inch rear end runs a nodular pumpkin with 4.88:1 gears and aftermarket axles. It's all hooked up to the homebuilt frame with an Art Morrison four-bar setup and coil-overs. The front end consists of a Model A axle and leaf spring, '40 Ford spindles, and split wishbones. The 17-inch American spindle-mount wheels on the front are offset by 8x15-inch Halibrand solids in the rear. The 1924 body is set back 25 percent and channeled the depth of the frame rails. A belly pan was added, and Chuck Blanchard stitched the seat in rolled and pleated vinyl as well as stitching up the traditional white tonneau cover for the cockpit. The paint is '56 Ford Golden Rod yellow, which matches the very-lowered '56 Ford F-100 pickup that serves as a push-car/truck. The 1,600-pound roadster runs 120 miles per hour in the low-11-second range.

A close-up shot of the Dodge Red-Ram hemi and the four alcohol-fed Stromberg carburetors.

I was in L.A. in 1996, shooting some features for a magazine, and I got together with my good friends Dennis Kyle, Bill Vinther, Don Small, and Cal Tanaka. To make a long story short, we were doing a garage tour of ongoing projects and we stopped by Cal's to see this front-engined dragster he had been talking about. It's a beauty and Cal said it was the "Tanaka and Brewer Racing" project. Danny Brewer is the engine builder, and what he's come up with so far is a 400-ci Chevy small-block with a Cosworth crank and pistons, Carrillo rods, Crower SS rockers, a Vertex magneto, and a set of Hilborn injectors. They set it up with a two-speed Powerglide and a Chrysler rear end with 4.11 gears and Airheart dual-spot brakes. The frame is chrome-moly steel and the full aluminum body was formed by Terry Hegman, a master at hand-crafting forms that have a beautiful visual and aesthetic balance. Cal bought the black-with-flames dragster from Bob Halock already painted. But, they weren't Cal's flames, and it wasn't his black, so he changed it. Cal also has an innate sense of visual design, which is probably why he picked up this front-engine "digger" when he had a chance. The rear wheels are Halibrand 15x10's with front-runner 17-spoke wheels. It is a beautiful style that is reminiscent of the beautiful and lethal Greer-Black-Prudhomme dragster in style and era.

Don Jackson's *Purple Haze* '32 Austin Bantam roadster is powered by a blown, bored and stroked, 1957 Chrysler 392 hemi engine. The final displacement rounds out to 468 cubic inches and he is running a Mooneyham 8-71 magnesium blower topped with a magnesium Enderle injection setup. A two-speed, air-shifted Lenco transmission and a Crower triple-disc clutch transfer all the horsepower back to a full-floating Ford 9-inch rear end. The car was originally built in 1964 and Don restored it in 1994. The best time and speed so far is 7.6 seconds at 195 miles per hour. The altered is very well detailed and finished. Dale Poore, a very creative and free-spirited Portland, Oregon, resident, laid out the flames and Mitch Kim lined in the striping.

The original Stone, Woods, and Cook '40 Willys, built in 1961, was powered by a 6-71 blown, four-port injected 394 Olds engine. The team ran Olds engines until 1964, when it converted to Chrysler hemis. The cars ran from 1961 to 1966, during what many of us think were some of the most exciting times in drag racing, the gasser wars. The matches between the Stone, Woods, and Cook team and Big John Mazmanian were legendary. K. S. Pittman was also racing a Willys back then and actually was part of the original team of Pittman/Stone/Woods. Mike Cook is Doug Cook's son, and is a highly regarded Bonneville and dry lakes land speed racer in his own right. Mike was given this '41 Willys coupe (a later version then the original 1940) by father Doug Cook and Tim Woods, who were 50/50 owners in the car when it was retired in 1967. He has since restored the car.

I photographed the Number 554 Mooneyham and Sharp '34 coupe at the Seattle International Raceway in 1990. At the time, Jerry Moreland owned the restored racer. He took it to Bob Bauder for the complete and accurate-looking restoration. An updated version of the 6-71 Mooneyham-blown and Hilborn-injected Chrysler 392 hemi engine is a direct drive to the solidly mounted Dana 4.10 rear end. The nitro load is limited 55 percent after the restoration, as there are still are a lot of "old" parts in the car. In the early 1950s the '34 coupe, originally built by Gene Mooneyham of Mooneyham blower fame, ran as a full-fendered car. By the mid-1950s, however, it had been reworked to appear as it does in this photograph, without fenders, and it was the car to beat in its class. This is one of the all-time nastiest record-holding coupes to run the drag-racing circuit.

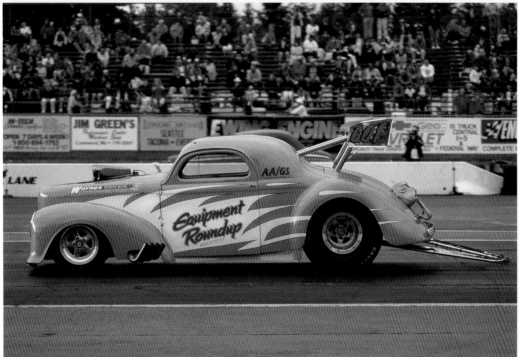

Another early blown gas coupe that was photographed while running at the Seattle strip in 1990 was the K. S. Pittman Willys. These cars are a handful to drive, and seeing them run is what I remember about the "golden" years of drag racing.

Wayne Harry driving the Equipment Roundup '40 Willys at the Seattle International Raceway in the mid-1990s. The gasser runs an alcohol-fed blown big-block Chevy. Wayne's Willys are highly competitive throughout the west in the nostalgic racing meets.

Far Left
The Champion Speed Shop dual-engine dragster was smoking the tires all the way down the Seattle International Raceway quarter-mile strip sometime during the mid-1990s. This exhibition rail never failed to put on a great show; I used to see this car at various gatherings in the Bay Area. Jim McLennan and his Champion Speed Shop in South San Francisco ran Chevy-powered fuel dragsters during the 1960s and owned the Half Moon Bay drag strip, where they had a tendency to dominate.

Left middle
Jack "The Bear" Coonrod's '33 Willys making a pass at Seattle International Raceway during the mid-1990s with a blown early 392 Chrysler hemi. Jack has since switched to a blown all-aluminum Donovan hemi in the old gasser.

Above
Tom and Tom Jr. Schiffilea built this '40 Willys four-door sedan in their shop, with Tom Jr. doing most of the construction. They are running a 550-ci Hilborn-injected Chevy big-block with a turbo 400 tranny and a Ford 9-inch rear end. The car looked impressive and I caught a couple of photos while I was photographing Tom Sr.'s '32 three-window coupe.

CHAPTER THREE

Paul and Marcia Wingfield are some of the nicest folks I've met in all the time I've been photographing hot rods and custom cars. They are having a very good time with this '34 Ford three-window coupe, which Paul started working on in 1997. He knew the look that he wanted, and he wanted a car that they could drive anywhere, and possibly do a little racing, which he has done also at the local drag strip in Spokane, Washington. I found that they were Pinehurst, Idaho, residents, which is about 2-1/2 hours north of where I call home. They have put over 15,000 miles on the car since it was finished and have been all over the West in it. He credits Tim Stromberger, of Tim's Hot Rods, in Greenacres, Washington, with a lot of help in the construction of the '34. They are running a TCI chassis and TCI independent front suspension with four-bar and Aldan coil-over setup in the rear with a Ford 9-inch. Paul decided on a 440-horsepower 502-ci Chevy big-block engine and a Doug Nash five-speed transmission. The 3-1/2-inch chopped Minotti body is finished in gloss black. Gracing the inside is a black tuck and roll leather and vinyl interior, accented with red piping. The polished American five-spoke wheels are perfect, as is the low and aggressive stance. It runs, and the 12-second times at the local strip in full street dress will attest to it.

STREET RODS

First a disclaimer or two: While I have titled it "Street Rods," I need to say by strict definition some cars in this chapter are hot rods. Selections were based on a traditional merit rather that the age-old question of whether the car is a "street rod" or a "hot rod." Purist street rodders and hot rodders may take exception with my criteria, but I believe my selections represent the genre.

Now for some historical perspective: Cotton Werksman and Paul Bruce Miller started the National Street Rod Association (NSRA) in 1970 with the idea that it would be a "low-key" club, on the national level, allowing all clubs a way to share common and mutual interests. There was to be no commercialism in the original concept. Tom Medley and *Rod & Custom* magazine, with Petersen Publications, became a sponsor of the first two national events. The first one was held in Peoria, Illinois, in 1970 with both Cotton and Bruce organizing and putting together the NSRA and the national event. The second national event was held in Memphis, Tennessee, in 1971, and was also sponsored by *Rod & Custom* magazine, under the direction of Tom Medley. Paul Bruce Miller had dropped out, leaving Cotton Werksman alone at the helm of the NSRA. Cotton teamed up with Vernon Walker and Gilbert Bugg, out of the Tennessee area, in 1971 or 1972 to help run the organization, and in 1972 Dick Wells, from Petersen Publishing, also became involved. Cotton left the organization sometime in the mid-1970s, feeling the whole thing had become far too commercial, and had moved away from the original concept. The NSRA became a business, whereas before, it was oriented more as a nonprofit organization that was providing a service to hot rodders throughout the country.

A couple of things happened during the early 1970s that had a cause and effect relationship on the culture. *Rod and Custom* magazine was disbanded by Petersen Publishing, and combined with *Hot Rod* magazine in 1972. This was at a time when the whole "street rod" movement and industry started to take hold. *Street Rodder* magazine, from McMullen Publishing, started publication in 1972 and became one of the leaders in the field of magazines representing the "hot rod culture," which was being transformed into a "street rod culture." NSRA became more oriented toward safety and acceptance by the general public and industry, rather than racing, and the organization worked to dispel the vaguely perceived "outlaw" image that hot rodding seemed to have.

Street racing was frowned upon, and NSRA members were urged to have their cars undergo safety inspections for official NSRA certification. Much of this was deemed a good thing, as it helped to make the hot rod sport/culture a much safer venue, but it also pushed it into the realm of acceptability, which tends to remove rough edges and raw creative flair. It's a double-edged sword; the hobby got safer and more acceptable, but it may have lost some of its edge, which can be regarded as good or bad, depending on your view.

It was at this point that hot rods and street rods seemed to take separate paths. Street rod design and construction were propagated from the industry of building street rods, i.e., a business. Hot rod traditionalists stayed away from fads and used original parts, or parts that were similar, to construct their cars. Street rod designs kept getting more and more exotic, and at times it was difficult to see the line separating custom-built exotic sports cars and street rods. Many had the same suspensions, and while bodies resembled earlier models, they sometimes were sculpted to the point of just barely resembling what they started as.

It was a natural progression, and it is progress in a manner of speaking, but it also changed most people's concept of what is a hot rod. That is where the terms "hot rod" and "street rod" seemed to go in different directions, with hot rods holding onto their racing and traditional heritage, and street rods allowing forays into the exotic realm of modern technology, materials, and designs. While there are cars in this area that are really hot rods, they may not be "traditional" hot rods, because they use certain modern technologies and designs.

Street rods combine a lot of different automotive realms that are sometimes hard to codify into certain categories, as so many of them have blended into mixtures and designs of their own. Such is the creative nature of the industry, which is constantly trying out new ideas and directions within the culture. It also says something about lost information, and as the original hot rod generation of the 1940s passes, then the 1950s, and then the 1960s, their information gets lost, gets passed on in different versions, or just gets watered down.

On the other side, the hobby also rises in sophistication and concept, so again it sometimes is a positive or negative thing, depending on perspective. Directions come in and out of fashion, and those that endure become classics. In the scope of history, hot rods are relatively new, so enthusiasts are just now starting to define what is important historically.

I'm not sure what would have happened to the hot rod culture if this had not all come about. I do believe that with the advent of the street rod culture and its increased popularity and acceptance, it has survived and prospered. It has changed somewhat, but all in all, it is healthy, and it still allows multiple directions and designs from within the culture. The idea of limiting change to "this direction" or "that direction," is ludicrous. The culture began open ended and should remain open minded. It just shouldn't rely of how much money you can pour into whatever it is that you are building. There will always be "good" examples, and "not-so-good" examples; perhaps it is in the mind of the beholder and can change from region to region. Personal taste inspires, and that which survives the test of time is what will continue to define the culture. Does industry lead the direction, or is industry reflecting what people want?

Gary Meadors, who was involved with the NSRA events, left in 1986 to form the Goodguys organization, which expanded the street rod gathering arena and directly competed with the NSRA in many cases. This gave the street rodder a multitude of "fairground type" events to attend throughout the year. These events became gathering points to show cars, as well as a place packed with others who shared the same interests. As the baby boomers started returning to the street rod culture, they found it had been "sanitized" somewhat, and that it was a good place to take the family. Between the Goodguys and the NSRA events, street rodders could choose the area of the country they wanted to visit.

The events kept building in popularity, with the NSRA National event (held at various locations ranging from Oklahoma to Kentucky and Ohio) reaching record numbers of cars and attendees. They have had as many as 13,000 cars registered for an event. These are all street rods, and it boggles the mind to think of actually trying to see them all in a four-day weekend.

The NSRA has a cut-off year of 1948 and would allow nothing later than that year, which has always been a source of debate. Many, however, believe the 1950s cars were part of the same culture, as they had grown up owning and modifying these cars. The Goodguys events expand the eligible years somewhat, often up into the 1960s cars, depending on the event and location. Many times the cut-off date has to do with the number of people attending. That is, adding the later model cars would add to the cars available in some areas. Many believed very strongly that eliminating some later cars, especially the 1949–1951 models, lost the classic custom car group.

Some of the emerging directions in street rodding include resto-rods, phantoms, prostreet, high-tech and/or billet, and exotic. I have included examples of most of these categories, but evolution and crossover designs produce unique and varied combinations, which even include the traditional or nostalgic cars. Resto-rods are just that, restored stock bodies with updated drivetrains, interiors, wheels, tires, and paint. During the early and middle 1970s, the resto-rod movement started blending with other styles, and street rodders started modifying the bodies and reevolving back into the hot rod/street rod genre. Street rods moved into the monochromatic Euro-look era, and with the introduction of billet aluminum parts, cars were created and worked into very smoothly designed street rods. These cars had a sense of craft and finish that paralleled, and often passed, those in the show car circuit. In fact, many of these cars ended up with some of the major awards.

This genre naturally blended with high-tech and what I would call the exotic class of street rods. These were cars with very high-performance "sports-car" suspension systems and coachwork that would compare with the fine European builders, sometimes using engines and drivetrains from the European cars they were being compared to. Street rods with independent rear ends, usually Jaguar or Corvette, became commonplace. Many aftermarket street rod suppliers started manufacturing independent front suspension systems, and when you combine all of this with the finely crafted billet pieces that were becoming readily available, you had a car that was quite different from what many of us had grown up with. Anyone could get on the phone, dial an 800 number and purchase a complete car in pieces and various states of completeness. The average street rodder, or street rodder "wannabe" could get into the culture/movement/sport with no prior experience. The popularity kept growing all through the 1980s and 1990s, and hasn't shown any sign of leveling off yet. This changed the movement and culture completely and a multitude of highly qualified builders and designers became well known for their cars and influence within the culture.

"Lil' John" Buttera and Boyd Coddington added their influence to the high-tech arena, and were the ones who inspired the high-tech street rod, along with well-known automotive designers such as Thom Taylor and Larry Erickson. The designers keep things on the edge and pointed toward the exotic. Chip Foose, who worked with Boyd Coddington for a time, is well known for his expertise in design, tending toward the smooth and more exotic style. His father, Sam Foose, also well known for his design and craftsmanship in car building, certainly influenced Chip's attention to design and expertise in the field. Troy Trepanier is a designer/builder known for his radical and very high-tech cars built during the 1990s and 2000s.

Designs and drawings from Darrell Mayabb, Steve Stanford, or even ink-slinger and well-known cartoonist Dave Bell, have influenced the overall scene and direction of street rod design. Tom Prufer's '34 Ford *Cop Shop Coupe* was inspired by a Dave Bell drawing in *Street Rodder* magazine, which headed one of their columns.

Steve Moal, another California builder from the Oakland area, is well known for his craftsmanship and expertise in car building, especially if it requires metal forming to a level of perfection seen in early coachwork craft. Roy Brizio in the San Francisco area has been building hot rods and street rods of the Northern California style. Pete Chapouris, and the SoCal Speed Shop in Southern California, are well known for building cars with a more traditional look. The thing is, all of these builders and designers have the ability to take these designs in any direction required. Each has his own style and area of expertise, and will tend toward these directions, but with the ever-changing styles and directions, it is hard to say where it will all end up.

The cost to build a complete "turn-key" and "drive it out of the shop" car can range from $75,000 to $500,000 depending on the amount of work involved. When a street rod reaches the upper end of the price scale, what separates it from cars in the exotic arena? The workmanship and overall design equals that of the great European builders and designers.

Perhaps some of this is responsible for the "nostalgic" movement, or a return to the roots of hot rodding. Street rods, and hot rods, are still being built in backyards and garages by average builders who cannot, and do not want to, enter the realm of the high-dollar car. Many builders still hold to the traditional ideals and have an aesthetic that's closer to the original history, which was discussed in Chapter One. People like Vern Tardel, Bill Vinther, or Pete Eastwood, all have a sense of this history, and each has an aesthetic vision of the culture, which is quite different from the high-tech or exotic design. Each arena is valid from different perspectives, and again, the variety is what keeps the culture active and alive.

The evolution of street rodding from traditional hot rodding pulls ideas in from many arenas, both inside and outside the original culture.

For example, Pro/Street cars tend toward the drag-racing style, with large rear tires emulating the huge drag slicks used in racing, fit under the body by "tubbing" the back rear wheel openings. These cars often had overbuilt full-race engines that were at times undrivable on the street, but the overall look included full roll cages and racing harnesses, which added to the safety of the driver. "Fat Jack" Robinson and Jerry Moreland created some cars in the mid-1980s that fit into this genre, but these cars were really full-on race cars that just happened to be street legal and have old Ford bodies; a '40 sedan in Moreland's case, and a '46 coupe in Robinson's. The look slowly evolved into a more "streetable" design, with engines and drivetrains that had been "detuned" to allow everyday driving.

The "phantom" class involves body styles that were never produced by the major automobile manufacturers. Some of these cars were "design improvements" that spun off originals, and some were designs that were extended into different years, such as a '34 Ford roadster pickup, a '34 Ford C-400 convertible sedan, a '32 Ford tudor phaeton, or a '32 Ford woodie/sportsman roadster. The Minotti 1937 Ford three-window coupe has been a popular model produced in fiberglass. Some of these were produced by the aftermarket street rod industry, and some were built and conceived by individuals as a personal idea or design direction.

I have included examples of these in the following pages, but evolution and crossover designs produce unique combinations, including even the traditional or nostalgic cars. Some of the cars in this chapter defy labeling, but as it is a close call all around, bear with it . . . enjoy the ride. I have also included a few cars from the 1950s and early 1960s, which were part of the movement, but what many refer to as street machines. Some of these are crossover cars, that I believe could be called street rods in their own right, with some stretch of definition. There is one exception, which is a perfect example of a Detroit factory-built hot rod, the 421 SD Pontiac Ventura, or Catalina. They are part of the culture and just represent a different genre.

The cars are listed in chronological order, or, by year of the car, rather than by which "type" of street rod it is. You can form your own opinions as to whether the car

Jim Longworth of Tacoma, Washington, owned this '28 tudor sedan in the early 1990s when I photographed it. It is a nice clean example of a monochromatic home-built car. All the frame construction, the four-bar setups front and rear, the top chop, the three-piece hood, the saddle gas tanks on each side, and the rear pan work were done and finished by Jim in his garage. The workmanship and attention to detail in this car are equal to a much more expensive pro-built version. Jim decided on a Chevy 283-inch engine for power followed by a turbo 350 transmission. There is nothing exotic here, but plenty of reliable power and very comfortable driving. The license plate at the time read "HOMEBLT," which it was.

This is another car from Don Audel's garage, and you could say that it's a little bit more refined than his '15 Model T. This '28 Ford Touring has had some amazing work done to it, and a lot of it is very subtle. Don had originally planned on this being a restoration project, but things changed as they so often do, and he went in a completely different direction. One of those things that does make this '28 phaeton so interesting, is that Don, in a very subtle way, changed the body by sectioning a wedge out of it, starting at the back with zero, and moving up to the front with a 2-1/2-inch cut at the radiator. He then stepped the front fenders 2 inches and wedge-cut the running board aprons to match. The hood top and cowl are one-piece with a hinge at the windshield. The whole thing lifts up to access the engine, the electrical system, and fuse panels all at once. There are many hand-formed parts on the car. Don is a master craftsman, creating the dash, windshield posts, steering wheel, bumpers, and the many brackets, fasteners, and knobs used in the car's construction. A polished aluminum louvered belly pan runs from the firewall to the front. The frame was hand-built of 2x4-inch rectangular tubing with help from Jim Evans and Jim Poppenroth. A Halibrand quick-change center section was added to a '40 Ford rear end, set up with a four-bar and spring, as is the Superbell 4-inch front axle. The McLean chrome spokes and the beautiful black paint, coupled with the very tasteful Mercedes gray vinyl interior, make this '28 Ford a winner. The proportioning on the body, with that wedge section cut out of it, is unique, and it makes the car.

Don Audel, and his son Hazen, put this 1928 phaeton together with parts sitting around the shop that were left over from the many and various projects, and Don's long history in the culture. The steel '28 Ford phaeton sits on a 2x6-inch rectangular tubing hand-built frame that has been pinched and tapered in the front; they styled the car to be late 1950s vintage. About the only things they had to purchase were the engine, transmission, tires, gauges, and the original '32 radiator, which they found at a local radiator shop. The rear end is a '48 Ford, as are all the brakes. They had a body man rough out the steel body, and Hazen then learned how to finish it, right up to the final paint, which he and Don sprayed. They narrowed a Superbell 5-inch dropped axle and split the wishbone, and added a stainless 28-gallon gas tank made by Jim Tipke and Bob Sparboro, who also crafted the stainless side-mounted headers. Don and Hazen made all the nerf bars, side bars, and the roll bar, polished it all themselves and just had the chrome shop dip them. They added a '32 Deuce grille and the "polish once a week" magnesium Halibrands, 5-inch on the front and 12-inch on the back. They finished it before Hazen graduated from high school. Hazen then entered it in the Spokane Auto Show where it took first place. It is a great father-and-son project, which Don hopes Hazen keeps as long as he (Don) has had his 1915 T roadster, which he built at about the same age.

Above right

Nick and Linda Cline sold a '39 Chevy coupe to make room for this steel '29 Ford roadster pickup in their garage. The pickup is all traditional street rod, running a 283-ci Chevy small-block and a turbo 350 transmission. The all-steel body is original, but the fenders, bed, and tailgate are Brookville roadster reproductions. A TCI frame supports everything, with a Super Bell 4-inch dropped axle and four-bar setup on the front and coil-overs on the rear.

I photographed Aaron Jeppson's '31 Ford roadster in a Lewiston, Idaho, gravel pit in the late 1980s. The roadster is a good example of street rods of that time, running a Jaguar rear end and Tru-Spoke wire wheels. Those wheels were popular during the 1970s and 1980s, especially on resto-rods, which this roadster isn't. Aaron was running a Chevy 350-inch engine with dual-fours and a turbo 400 transmission. Other modifications include a chopped Carson-style top, milled windshield posts, Rootlieb hood, and a '32 grille.

I photographed Irene and Don Richardson's chopped, channeled, and flamed black '33 Ford pickup at the Goodguy Northwest Nationals in Puyallup, Washington, sometime in the mid-1990s, along with a '50 Ford custom business coupe owned at the time by Steve Buhr. Both cars work together and both are very retro. Irene's '33 was originally built in 1959 and passed through a few owners before Eric Perkins got it. Irene and Don bought the truck from Eric and freshened it up, and got it to sit right, as in lowering. The flames were added in the 1990s and the truck continues to be used and driven. Don and Irene own and run Richardson's Custom Auto Body in Hoquiam, Washington.

Left bottom

I photographed this group of Northwest cars in Lewiston, Idaho, sometime in the mid-1990s in the parking lot behind a Kentucky Fried Chicken. Everybody was getting ready to take off, and it was the only place we could find quickly. Larry Foss' '31 Ford tudor sedan, which has gone from brother to brother to brother in the Foss family; John Wagers' '40 Ford coupe deluxe, which he has had since 1960; and Irene and Don Richardson's '33 Ford pickup make up the group. These folks travel together often and are seen all over the West. That's what it's about, right? All of these cars have a long Northwest history.

Right

Dave and Laura Elliot's dark Ferrari-green '32 tudor sedan is beautifully finished. The chassis and suspension were built and assembled by Pete Eastwood. He set up the '57 Ford 9-inch rear with ladder bars and a transverse spring, then used a stainless four-bar, transverse spring, and dropped axle on the front. The 355-ci Chevy engine and 2.02 heads were blueprinted and assembled by Jerry Finkelstein. The stock-height all-steel body is pretty much the same as it came from the factory, except for smoothed drip rails, shortened rear bumper brackets, taillight brackets, and dropped headlight bar. John Carambia sprayed the beautiful green paint, and Jim Bailey covered the interior with gray leather. The '32 tudor is a beautiful example of a recently built "resto-rod." It even still has the top insert.

145 Street Rods

Claude and Susan Freund's '32 Ford highboy roadster was the "Sweepstake Roadster Winner" in the 1997 Portland Roadster Show. They both have been around the hot-rod culture for some time, and they put this roadster together and loaded it with hot-rod goodies. Claude has been building roadsters since he was 13 years old. He's in his early 50s now, so count the years as he has some experience. Tim's Hot Rods in Spokane, Washington, pinched the frame and "bobbed" the horns, then added the custom cross-members. Claude threw a B&M blown 350 Chevy small-block and a Halibrand quick-change rear end into the mix and finished the Wescott body off with a rolled pan and retractable rear license. The Frank Geis–built three-piece hood was hand-formed to accommodate the blower scoop, as was the floorpan for the Halibrand third-member. They threw in a set of Halibrand wheels, had Frank Geis also lay some three-dimensional flames on the bright orange paint, and then had George Frank add a French vanilla vinyl interior. It all works, and judging from the awards, including the Magnum Axle Real Hot Rod Award in Puyallup, others like it as much as the Freunds.

Far left bottom
This is one of those "phantom" hot rods that, at one time, helped foster the rumor that Henry Ford actually did build one, only deciding not to put it into production in 1932. Rick and Brenda Davis, out of Chilliwack, British Columbia, did all they could to continue the legend by buying the phaeton, which was a very nicely put-together car that came out of a '32 tudor sedan. Regan Schewchuk actually did the conversion to the steel body and sold it as a "resto-rod." When Rick and Brenda got the car, they rebuilt it their way, using only the body, top, frame rails, grille shell, and axle. Rick originally used a chopped original windshield, and decided to freshen it up with a Duvall, both of which had full folding tops. The 355-ci Chevy small-block runs with a Dyers 4-71 blower on it, which has logged over 50,000 reliable miles. The Reimer wire wheels complete the look and the two-door phantom looks great with the top up or down. Rick and Brenda also have a full set of side curtains for it in case of inclement weather, which sometimes happens in the Northwest. Rick also has a full set of fenders and running boards for the car, which I've seen on the car in photographs. Rick and Brenda run a photography studio, and the photographs looked as good as the car did with the fenders on.

Chuck McCoy, of Bellingham, Washington, owns this '32 Ford roadster, and it fits in the hot-rod, high-tech, pro-street class. The workmanship is impeccable, with much of it being done by the owner and John Barbero of Pyramid Auto Engineering in Bellingham. The bodywork on the steel Brookville body was handed off to Al Swedberg in Centralia, Washington, as were the hood and hood sides. The suspension is all custom, with the owner-built four-bar and diagonal link system and Aldan double-adjust coil-overs, with a custom antisway bar system for the rear holding the Mark Williams 9-inch Ford 4:11 rear end. The front end is a stainless custom Kugel Komponents independent. The real eye-catchers on this roadster are the injector tubes sticking out of the hood, which are Ron's Racing staggered stacks connected to an electronic computerized fuel-injection system by BDS (Blower Drive Service). The '98 Chevy 509-ci Gen VI CNC bowtie block is running a Lunati roller cam, 11.7:1 compression, and GM aluminum CNC heads, ported. It was all put together by Tyler King at High Performance Racing Engines in Lynden, Washington, and it puts out 750 horsepower and 700 ft-lb of torque. Chuck McCoy and John Barbero did all the custom exhaust and had it coated at Performance Coatings in Auburn, Washington. Frank Marino sprayed the PPG 1998

Mercedes Smoke Silver paint and Mitch Kim laid down some lines. Chuck then finished off the look with ET 10-spoke 15x6-inch wheels on the front and 15x14-inch ET III's on the rear. The Mercedes parchment-and-black upholstery, installed by Dan's Custom Interiors in Kelowna, British Columbia, Canada, matches the custom owner-built billet-aluminum and carbon-fiber dash.

Left

Frankie DeMarco started with a '32 Wescott roadster body, chopped windshield, and a Roy Brizio Stage III chassis, then he and Cal Tanaka hammered the thing together in 18 days and nights. Frankie owns El Monte Auto Paint in El Monte, California, so obviously, he supplied the custom purple mix that he sprayed on the car. The roadster is running a 350/350 Chevy combination with the engine being one of the ZZ1 345 horse crate motors. Cal did a lot of the fit and finish on the setup.

Above

I photographed Steve Heller's beautiful smooth and low '32 Ford highboy roadster up in the hills outside of Pleasanton in the early 1990s after running into it in the Goodguys' West Coast Nationals. Steve and Joanne Heller owned the car and were enjoying driving it all over the West at the time. He has since moved back to Florida, which he believes has better roadster weather and, he says, better roads. Steve traded a '30 two-door phaeton for this car at the L.A. Roadster Show and only found out later who really built the car. That person was A. L. Shurtz of Bullhead City, Arizona. Shurtz started building the car in 1985 and based the car on a '32 frame that he had kicked up in the back with a Model A cross-member and spring. He pinched the front rails and added a raised T-bucket-styled spring perch. He located a fiberglass body and added all his own metal and wood bracing, while at the same time smoothing the inside and outside of the body, rounding the door corners, and smoothing out the deck lid area. He smoothed the cowl area and fashioned the windshield out of 3/16-inch strap iron and 5/16-inch square tubing with one side cut off. In the 2-1/2 years following the build, Shurtz racked up 42,000 miles on the car driving it all over the Southwest. Since Steve has owned it, the odometer passed the 50,000 mark in the early 1990s. Steve also added the louvered hood sides and the wide whitewall tires, as A. L. Shurtz was running it with blackwalls, Moon discs, and open hood sides.

I photographed this '32 roadster highboy in Puyallup quite a few years ago, when Cam Grant owned it, in the middle of a pouring rainstorm. We kept ducking under cover during the downpours, and running out to get a few shots when it let up. The car was showing the Duvall windshield that Cam and Gary Lang were producing at the time, and they were fairly new to the market. Gary Lang's '36 roadster also had one, and both cars were getting their fair amount of coverage. Both were very clean examples.

Above

Bob and Jan Lindeman bought this '33 Ford roadster as a finished car, and being that Bob has a chopped '33 coupe of his own, this one is Jan's car. He also gives total credit to Tom Arnold for conceiving the car, which he claims was inspired by a car built in 1938 by Wes Collins. Tom lined up Gary Sutherland to do the chassis work and had Ron Moses build a Chevy 383-inch stroker engine with 2.02 heads. He lined up Larry Foss to take care of the fit and finish of the Wescott body, and to spray it with acrylic lacquer black paint. He then had Ken Jones chop the original '33 top bows 3 inches, to match the Duvall windshield, and finish the rest of the interior in Mercedes Benz dove-gray leather. The '39 banjo steering wheel and column, and the original Auburn dash and gauges add to the classic, early inspired look.

Jim Westrick's '34 Ford roadster is a Wescott-bodied, Chevy 350 small-block-powered very straightforward street rod. The roadster was built by Bob Burley in Portland, Oregon, who C'ed the frame to help it ride better, and set up the suspension with a four-bar and 4-inch dropped axle front with a 9-inch Ford with coil-over springs in the rear.

Right top
It is not often that you will see a '34 two-door woody phaeton. In fact, it's the only one that I have seen, which is probably due to the fact that it is a phantom car thought up and built by Greg Rice, in Post Falls, Idaho. He started with a four-door cowl and floor pan, making the rest from square tubing and wood. He added a '32 fold-down roadster windshield and stretched the rear end out 14 inches to get the proper proportions. Greg decided on a 322-ci Buick Nailhead engine, mating it to an early Ford open drive and an 8-inch Ford rear end. Greg boxed the frame for stability and added a 4-inch dropped axle with a split wishbone configuration. An original '34 four-door front seat goes well with the Dodge Caravan seat that was adapted for the rear. This car has a real touch of the old, and it looks like it was released by Ford.

Neil Brislawn bought this '36 three-window well-chopped coupe from Eric Perkins, who discovered the car behind a filling station in Indiana in 1973. He picked the car up for a pricey sum of $100, although at the time it was in primer, and lacked an engine and interior. Eric brought it back to the West and started reworking the chassis, where he added a Corvette front and rear suspension, which gave the car, even as low as it is, full-turning radius and suspension travel, at least until the bottom of the car hits the ground. Neil bought the car at that time, with it still needing an engine and interior. The engine he chose was a well-warmed '70 Chevy 396, bored .030 over, which conservatively puts out about 425 horsepower. Brislawn used a '36 seat, updating it with six-way power and allowing it to move back into the package tray area, which gives an incredible amount of leg room. The bumpers are from his brother, who owns Bumpers by Briz. Neil has since added flames on the car, as well as wide whitewall tires and 1950s' era spinner caps, and he drives the car everywhere. I've seen it up and down the West Coast at different times all through the 1990s and just last summer at Puyallup, Washington.

Above left

Jack and Velva Aiken purchased this car from Bob Livingston in the Portland, Oregon, area. The 2-inch chopped top is an original working convertible top. The body is a fiberglass reproduction made by Pat Mooney, but all of the rest is original steel. The front suspension is Mustang II, which helps the overall ride. The engine is a Ford 289 small-block backed by a C4 Ford automatic. Dale Withers applied the black lacquer paint, and all that the Aikens needed to do was drive the retro-looking, yet modernized roadster, which they have, to the tune of over 16,000 miles in the first few years.

I photographed this '36 Ford Woody at Pleasanton in the mid-1990s when Larry Anderson owned the car. He got the car from Robert Livingston, who did the actual restoration and upgrading. It was Robert who found a body-tag off the car that told him that this was Number 6 of that year's production, which makes it a special find. Robert replaced the '36 frame with a '37 frame, because the original had been severely damaged by a leaky battery. He also replaced the drivetrain with a complete '40 unit, adding a Chassis Engineering dropped axle. The stock '40 engine is covered with Thickstun parts, including a twin two-barrel carburetor setup and Thickstun marine air cleaner. He then sold the car to Larry Anderson, who sold the car to Richard Munz, who had the flathead rebuilt by Roger Gregg, a veteran flat-head expert. Gregg Roger bumped the stock engine up to 276-cubic-inches with a 3-5/16-inch bore and a Mercury crank, added some Jahns pistons and an Isky three-quarter-race cam, and covered the iron heads with the same Thickstun "boat covers." Richard has a beautiful example of one of Henry's best years.

Right top

Mark Cain is a builder out of the Bremerton, Washington, area. All the work on the '37, obviously, comes out of his shop, which is Cain's Customs. He constructed the '37 Ford sedan convertible for himself, and it's perfect. The very tasteful dark blue paint, red wheels, and stance make this car. Mark likes his cars low to the ground and as he drives them, he built this to be functional with the full, slammed, stock-bodied appearance. He kept the folding top fully functional and the stock-appearing interior, which was stitched up by his mother in gray leather, fits with the overall visual appearance of the '37. This is a classic car that will not get old through the years.

Left bottom
Don and Jerinne Audel's '37 Ford tudor "flatback" sedan was built for comfort and reliability. Don set the front suspension up with a Chrysler K-car torsion bar, and parallel leaf springs in the rear, and put in a 350 Chevy small-block and a turbo 350 transmission. He also helped George Frank with the upholstery, which was laid on some 1994 Saturn seats, and sprayed the outside with a custom aqua mix of acrylic lacquer. The car is a sweet driver, and the contrast between the aqua paint and the red wheels, which were shod with wide whitewalls, is stunning and yet very straight-forward. The car is filled with all the creature comforts, such as a good heater, air conditioning, and power windows, all to Jerinne's specs.

How often do you see a '38 Cadillac opera coupe, much less one that has been pro-streeted? Janey and Tom Benson have had the car since 1961, when they purchased it in North Dakota for $65. There were only six of these made with side-mount spares. During Janey and Tom's ownership, they have had parts stolen off the car, and in fact, had the complete car stolen in 1970, and it sat in a sheriff's impound yard for eight years before being reunited with the Bensons. At that point, Tom commenced to completely rebuild the car into what you see in the photograph, a very rare pro-streeted Cadillac coupe, powered by a blown Chevy big-block. Tom constructed the chassis out of 2x 4-inch rectangular tubing and fitted a narrowed Chevy Nova front suspension to it. Tom estimates the horsepower at about 700 and at first it twisted the stock 31-spline Ford 9-inch axles, so he replaced them with a Dutchman alloy pair. The rear end is suspended and connected with a four-bar assembly, coil-overs, and a Watt's link connecting the narrowed rear to the frame. The interior is outfitted with T-Bird seats and a late-model Corvette dash.

Phil Huff, of Hailey, Idaho, has owned this '39 Ford coupe since he was 13 years old, back in 1961. He bought it with a "frozen" '48 Merc flathead under the hood, so he replaced it with a Chevy 283 and a four-speed transmission. When Huff rebuilt the car in the 1990s, he chopped the top 3 inches, redid the paint and interior, and replaced the 283 with a 327-inch small-block and fuelie heads. The car is a clean example of how well a top-chop on a difficult top can look. I photographed the coupe in Hailey, just outside of Ron Jolliffe's Rocket Science Engineering Garage, in the middle of February. It was five below zero and getting colder by the minute, as the sun had just gone down.

This '30 Deluxe Ford tudor sedan was built over 20 years ago by Longview, Washington, resident Chuck Miller. Jim Westrick now owns the car, and the black paint shows off the superstraight body, which is powered by a B&M supercharged 350-inch Chevy small-block. The car is bone stock on the outside and inside and a fine example of what is thought of as a "resto-rod."

This '39 Ford convertible sedan came up to Canada in the 1960s, and shortly thereafter Cam Grant first saw the car. He had always wanted one and thought about buying it then, but ended up waiting some 20 years before he actually purchased it. Cam had partnered with Gary Lang in a small company called Past Tech—they were the ones who started producing the repop Duvall windshields. The company has since been sold a couple of times. It was at this time that Cam was able to come up with the cash to buy the '39. The Mustang II front suspension and small-bock Ford engine had already been done when Cam got the '39, so all he had to do was replace the top, and put on some big and little wide whitewall tires. With a little massaging to the front suspension, the tires brought the car down to an appreciated level. The paint is rubbed through in spots from polishing, but that's the way Cam likes it and he has no plans on paint it. The car is a classic, and with the fact that only 3,561 of them were made in 1939, it's a keeper.

Terry Hegman's '39 Ford Deluxe coupe originated somewhere in Georgia. Henry Koenig bought it in pieces and brought it up to the Milwaukee area, where he put it back together as a show car, and only drove it 25 miles in 14 years. Henry sold the car to Dick Jutilla, who made a few changes, but only added 475 more miles on the car. Randy Hallman picked the '39 up at that point and took it back to the 1950s, so to speak. He added a dropped axle, stock-looking 15-inch steel wheels, and big and little wide whitewall tires. This is where Terry got hold of it. He traded his Deuce roadster for the '39 coupe and brought it back to Southern California. That's when I heard about it through a friend, Dennis Kyle. I arranged to photograph the coupe on my next trip to the L.A. area and did so, which was for a magazine feature at the time. The car had already, and recently, been photographed by somebody else for the same magazine, when it was still owned by Randy Hallman, and when it was still back East. Nonetheless, here is one of the shots we that we did that evening. The flathead-powered '39 is a beautiful example of its era.

Jim Westrick, and his son Mark, know how to deal with prime '40 Fords, especially a Folkstone Gray (tan) convertible and a Mandarin Maroon deluxe coupe, both of which were restored beauties. All they did was add dropped axles; reverse the spring-eyes front and back to get the ride height perfect; and add 15-inch wheels, 5-inch in the front and 7-inch in the back, with wide whitewall tires mounted on them. Of course the wheels did get painted red, and, oh yes, there is the dual exhaust. But that's really it. The restored cars were that nice when they picked them up. I literally fell all over myself photographing these two '40s. They're quite beautiful, just the way they are.

157 Street Rods

Steve Lemmons' '40 coupe has had a few owners, and it has been through some times, both good and bad, being at one time used as a high school car by one of the previous owner's kids. John Buttera bought the car at one point for his wife, and she drove it as a stocker for a couple of years before selling it to Brian Burnett of Los Gatos, California. He had Lem Toliver convert it to modern running gear and actually did some racing with it. It at one time had a 13.5 to 1 engine in it with an NOS bottle in the trunk. Lem Toliver then bought the car, putting in a Chevy 350 and a turbo 350 transmission, before he sold the car to Denny Leon of Gilroy, who added the underdash air conditioning. Jim Fergus traded an almost new Corvette for the '40. In 1987 Jim decided that he wanted a five-window coupe and had found one, so he called Steve, who had since told him he was interested in the car, and sold it to him. Since Steve has owned it, the engine has been rebuilt and Steve has generally detailed it, added a Chassis Engineering rear spring kit, and the American five-spokes. It still has the Dulux paint and the mohair interior. I photographed the '40 at the Wendover Airport in 1998 during Speedweek.

Below
Bill Woodworth's '40 Willys pickup is a pro-built car, all the way. Steve McGee built the B&M Megablown 427-ci Chevy big-block, and the one thing Bill was concerned about was that it would have too much horsepower, especially for the street. Steve McGee is well known in the dragrace world for his engine building. They backed the engine with a pro-built aluminum Powerglide and a Halibrand Champ rear end. Dale Withers, a Northwest builder outside of Portland, Oregon, is well known for his craftsmanship in construction and painting, especially black. He worked his magic on the Willys, doing the many modifications that were needed to get it to the stage you see in the photograph. The rear bead was raised and shortened and the rear fenders were raised, lengthened, widened, and re-turned so they would fit the big 15x14-inch Halibrand wheels and the 18.50x31-inch Mickey Thompson tires. The front Halibrand spindle-mounts were mounted on a Mustang II front end that Jack Slavik had remachined to fit them. The interior is fully caged and the upholstery is subtle gray leather. Dale Withers' black paint is flawless, as is the work underneath it.

Far right
Kay and Gary Harm's '46 Ford convertible had only 34,639 miles on the odometer when I photographed the car in Spokane, Washington, and that, folks, is the original mileage. They purchased the car from a cousin of the original owner with everything in the car that came with it new, including the owner's manual, factory toolkit, and jack. Gary repainted the original Moonstone Gray with Sikkins polyurethane. He louvered an extra hood, and rolled out the complete original front suspension and replaced it with a 4-inch dropped axle, Durant monoleaf spring, and a heavy Weedetr antiroll bar. Everything that Gary has replaced on the car has been saved, such as the front suspension and the plastic dash trim, which was replaced with new chrome pieces. The top was redone with Hartz cloth, and a LaBarron-Bonney kit replaced the original interior upholstery. At present the engine and drivetrain is completely stock, but Gary has all the parts to replace it with a 284-inch flathead. The flathead will run with a Scot supercharger and dual Stromberg 97 carburetors and the necessary vintage speed equipment to complement it. The '46 convertible looks brand new, because it almost is.

159 Street Rods

This very much lowered '46 Ford club coupe is owned by Tom Shall out of the Bay Area, California, whom I used to run into at many of the Goodguys' Events on the West Coast in the early 1990s. The ET mags and the ride height make this car. I always liked the car, possibly because my very first car was one of the same, a black $75 coupe bought when I was 15 years old.

Right middle

Mark and Joe Eddy picked up this '46 sedan delivery in undented, nonrusted, and generally very good condition, with "Visalia Potato Sales" still painted on the sides. Mark is a believer of building only drivers. The delivery has since been fully painted in Eddy's Beige (off white) and Cal Tanaka purple scallops striped in red. When I photographed it in 1994, up in the Pleasanton, California, hills, it was in original black and red-oxide primer, which covered the reworked areas. The "potato" logo had to go. It was replaced with "Eddy's Rod Shop," which they run in Temple City, California. The front axle assembly was replaced with a Mustang II independent and the Ford 9-inch rear was set in place with parallel leaf springs. A warmed Chevy small-block 350-ci engine and a turbo 350 transmission completed the drivetrain. Drive it they have, running the odometer well over 50,000 miles.

I run into Don Palfreyman, usually in the company of Mickey Ellis, every year at Bonneville. This '47 tudor sedan is a regular out there and that is where the car was photographed. Don has had the car for some time and has been reworking it into a new look year by year. He first added the purple paint, then the flames by his good friend Mickey Ellis, and then the wide whitewall tires, chrome wheels, and Mercury caps. The last time I had seen the car, it had aluminum wheels and blackwalls. The '47 looked good, but the new wheels and tires really made it come alive. The car is all Ford, with a 302-ci engine, C-4 transmission, and an 8-inch Ford rear end.

Tom Erickson reworked this '47 Ford woody with a Mustang II front suspension, a small-block Chevy engine and tranny setup, a Ford 9-inch rear end, a set of American Torque Thrust wheels, and a 600-watt stereo. He says the car is "a whole lot of fun." I photographed the wood car at Puyallup beside Dave Tarvin's yellow Model A coupe.

Len Bush bought this '48 Ford woody in 1975. He drove it until 1982, when he started tearing it down for a rebuild. It didn't get finished until 1991, when it made its "rebuilt" maiden voyage. Len moved from Spokane, Washington, to L.A. and back to Spokane during that time, which he says is the reason it took so long. Len decided a Chevy 327-inch engine with dual-fours would be a perfect match for a 350 turbo-hydro and Nova parallel sprung rear end. He was running a 4-inch dropped axle when I photographed it, but said he was thinking about putting in a Mustang II front suspension.

I photographed Dan and Kathryn Mycon's '48 Chevrolet Fleetline in Spokane, Washington, during the mid-1990s NSRA Northwest Nationals. We went to a warehouse district at the end of the day for the session, and as I was photographing, this sodium light turned on and lit the area with an eerie green light. It worked. Dan and Kathryn put in a Mustang II front suspension, updated the drivetrain with small-block Chevy parts, left on all the trim and drove it, after Dan painted it with "Mycon" purple and Porsche gray.

Laurie Peterson's '53 Studebaker is a "Champion Starliner Regal Hardtop" model. Laurie is out of North Vancouver, British Columbia, Canada, and he put together this pro-street version of a car that he's always loved. The 468-ci Chevy big-block is an LS6 version with aluminum Brodix-2 heads, a Comp cams roller unit, an Edelbrock Victor Jr. with an 830 annular Holly, and a Moroso crank-trigger ignition. The turbo -400 transmission is equipped with a 10-inch 4000 stall converter and a transbrake. The engine and tranny are tied in with an Art Morrison engine plate and midplate. The 9-inch Ford posi rear end is using Mosser Engineering axles and is held steady with ladder bars. The rear clip is an Art Morrison unit, and the front suspension is TCI. Laurie put in a 12-point roll cage, shaved the door handles, the hood and the trunk, and did all the suspension work. The only things he shopped out were the paint and interior. He crafted the 2-1/8-inch headers and the 3-inch exhaust, as well as doing all his own wiring. The car runs on pump gas and has run 11.22 at 124 miles per hour at the drag strip through the mufflers. Laurie is looking for 10s and says the car is driven all over, to all possible meets and drags.

Remember the two Westrick 1940s a little earlier in the chapter? Well, this '50 Oldsmobile 88 coupe owned by Steve Lemmons is of the same ilk, and he is from the same town, Longview, Washington. The "only" downside with the Olds, was that Steve purchased it in pieces, as it had been blown apart for a restoration/rebuild by the previous owner, Jim Donovan. Jim's widow, Jeannie, sold the car and a fair collection of extra and new NOS parts to Steve after Jim's untimely passing. Everything in this car is original and the car is flat-out gorgeous, thanks to the talents of Dale Withers, whom Steve hired to put everything back together and, essentially, finish the car. Dale applied one of his trade-mark black paint jobs and talked Steve into shorter springs and dropped spindles to give it a better looking ride height. Steve decided on Olds Fiesta spinner hubcaps to give it a true 1950s look. The Olds was photographed in the same session as the two '40s, obviously at the same location. It is a classic and perfect trio of lightly altered resto-rods.

Far left top

I don't know anything about this Plymouth station wagon, other than it was a one of the Pleasanton West Coast National Events in the mid-1990s. I was walking around the event with Bill Vinther, Paul Bos, Don Small, Gary Welter, and Cal Tanaka. Cal has this thing about really slammed (lowered) cars, and I grew up in one of these, so both of us were going nuts over this bone-stock lowered, rubbed-through green paint '53 station wagon. The rest of the group just looked at us as if we were nuts, but did quietly mention that it was "cool," at least in a sense. The other thing is that Cal is a surfer . . . and this wagon would make one right-on and properly subtle surfer car. It also ran absolutely quiet. We didn't even realize it was running until we were right next to it. Cal wanted the car, and I wanted it, but neither of us had the loose cash. When I was young, we traveled all over the West in one of these. I can even remember driving through Death Valley in it with a desert water bag hanging on the front.

Far left bottom

When Jim Westrick picked up the '55 Chevy 210 sedan, it had been bouncing around garages in Longview, Washington, as an unfinished project for some time. Jim traced the car's history back to 1968, when it was sectioned 4 inches. The top had also been chopped, but Jim couldn't fit in the car with it the way that it was, so he swapped tops with another '55 to bring it back to normal height. His son, Mark, was the one who really got it back on the road, adding a "lively" 454-inch Chevy big-block, a turbo 400, and a Ford 9-inch rear end. The car is tubbed in back to fit the big rear tires, caged in the interior to be safe, and painted a nice stock-looking '56 Cadillac Gulf Green and '55 Chevy India Ivory. The side trim has been airbrushed on.

Left

Gary Solomon, of Post Falls, Idaho, took this '55 Nomad and turned it into a pro-street race car, with a 10-point Art Morrison roll cage and all. The engine, and complete car for that matter, specs like a full-out race car. The 454-ci Chevy big-block has been bored, stroked, balanced, and o-ringed, and it runs a Chet Herbert full roller cam setup. The heads are ported and polished, and the induction is taken care of with an 8-71 Littlefield blower and twin Dominator carburetors. The double-disc hydraulic clutch is scatter shield encased and followed with a Doug Nash five-speed transmission. The exhaust escapes through a custom header set, 3-1/2-inch pipes, and FlowMaster mufflers. Everything is polished and finished, inside, outside, and underneath, and the Nomad body looks basically stock, until you see the blower, tubbed rear wheels, and caged interior. Gary added a Camaro front clip and had to recess the firewall to allow the 3-3/4-inch setback on the engine. The 3.50 Currie Brothers 9-inch rear end runs a Detroit Locker, Strange axles, and disc brakes, all set in place with an adjustable ladder bar with centering link suspension setup. The car is a little "lumpy" sounding, to say the least.

Left
This '61 Impala "bubbletop" was built from a restored original brought down from Canada by Steve's Auto Restorations in Portland, Oregon. The goal statement reads, "Modified for looks and performance, this car was constructed for use on the street as well as the drag strip. A 'built for business' attitude hides all but the obvious." It works, as the only things you really notice at first glance are the BDS 8-71 blower and dual Holley 850 carburetors sticking out of the hood. Now, how subtle can that be? Then you start to pick up on the other "hints," such as the Halibrand 15x7-inch front and 15x10.5-inch rear knock-off kidney bean wheels, the roll cage, and the 3-inch exhaust exiting in front of the rear wheels, where the body and frame have been carefully notched. The roll cage is painted to blend in with the very subtle and tastefully executed interior, and the competition seatbelt and harness setup barely shows, as do the competition Auto-meter gauges. The light-colored leather interior contrasts tastefully with the very understated and elegant candy green over black paint. When you start reading the specs, things start to come together. The stock frame has been plated with 5/16-inch sheet steel. An additional rear cross-member and plate have been added, along with stiffening plates on the front and rear of front cross-members and a boxed transmission mount for the Doug Nash five-speed. Then there is the trussed 9-inch Ford rear end with 3:50 Lennco locker and 35-spline axles and the 1-inch sway bars, front and rear. The engine is a Bowtie CNC tall-deck 477-ci Chevy block with Merlin heads. The car runs; I've seen it make a pass on the SIR dragstrip, just outside of Seattle.

Ron and Judy Ennis owned the '61 Chevy Impala "bubbletop" when I photographed it in Puyallup, Washington, in 1994. The 468-ci Chevy big-block with a roller cam and 10:1 compression woke me up one morning in the motel where I was staying. This is another example of a pro-street car as the rear wheel areas have been tubbed for the big 15x14-inch wheels and 31.50x18.50 tires, with the fronts only being 15x5-inch wheels and what are called "front-runner" tires. The mint green Impala is combined with an Art Morrison frame and ladder bars with coil-overs holding the 4:56 Ford 9-inch in place. No front inner fenderwells, just big-tube fenderwell headers in their place. The interior is set up with a full roll cage and competition gauges and is quite tastefully done in confetti gray burlap.

Right
Dick Uhlenkott's '61 Pontiac Ventura is a classic example of Detroit's early 1960s version of American muscle, or a late-model factory street rod. I must confess, if I had a choice between this, or one of the new American factory "street rods," it would win, hands down. This is an original '61 Pontiac Ventura 421 Super Duty, and Pontiac only released approximately 10 of the 421 engine SD "kits" to various places around the country. The "kits" were only available as over-the-counter (OTC) service package parts only and not available on production assembly vehicles. This is a factory race car, with the original four-speed transmission and the 4:11 Posi-Traction rear end. The engine was very conservatively rated at 373 horsepower, with the very same engine being rated at 405 horsepower the following year. It also has the correct eight-lug wheels.

167 Street Rods

CHAPTER FOUR

I first saw Ken and Cindy Wells' '50 Buick Sedanette in Puyallup, Washington, in the early 1990s running with an original Buick straight-eight engine. He has since then changed the drivetrain and frame-clips, front and rear, to '72 Buick configuration, tied together in the middle with 2x5-inch frame rails. He kept the car low, very low, and was talking about painting it gloss something, but the last time I saw it, the custom mix blue with flattener was still on it. When I photographed it, Ken had 120 louvers in the hood following the curve lines, the headlights and taillights had been frenched, and the body had been shaved of all trim and handles. The Moon discs are perfect, and Cindy did the upholstery work, so both of them have sweat equity built into the car. This is a "cruising mystery" photograph taken one night at the Pleasanton West Coast Nationals, sometime in the mid- to late 1990s.

Denny Hall's '51 Mercury, taken during the summer of 2000.

CUSTOMS

I asked Dick Page if he would write down some of his observations about the custom car side of the culture, and he did just that. I have known Page for some time, and have always respected his views on hot rods and custom cars. This photograph was taken in Page's shop over 10 years ago, and it is one of my favorites, as it epitomizes the actual work involved in creating a custom car. It shows the craftsmanship required to physically change or remodel the automobile by adding the creative, or artistic side of customizing. It involves many of the same elements that are used in any visual art, such as form, shape, pattern, texture and color, all used in conjunction with the principles of design. These design principles, such as dominant feature, proportion, balance, perspective, and visual rhythm, when used judicially, produce something on the visual side of our perception that sparks an aesthetic response, or a positive reaction. In some circles, it is called "gut reaction."

Page and I have talked about artistic correlations in car customizing, and he has offered some opinions and stories. I believe they are worth listening to and I definitely place a lot of value on his experience and knowledge. The thing is, I've seen what Page has done, and I happen to like and agree with what I've seen. Page has written articles for various publications, and actually ran a regional Northwest television show on the car culture. He's been around for a while, and he's paid his dues. It also should be noted, that he teaches a vocational technology course at Foss High School in the Tacoma, Washington, area, so he is passing this information along to some very fortunate students.

It's Why We Do What We Do . . .

The *Blue Book of Custom Restyling*, a Dan Post vintage publication, copyright 1944, revised 1952, is a great example of early remodeling text. It encouraged the reader to invoke a "natural sense of design and balance."

Stock production automobiles are a compromise between the stylist and production engineers, with some advertising input thrown in. Since the original contours often show a lack of inspiration, a good custom can yield a distinct improvement in style and grace. Post's text goes on to say that every car is subject to optical illusions, some good, some bad. Customizing, if it is to be successful, according to Post, should highlight the finer values and camouflage the less attractive ones. The book is hard to find but recommended reading for anyone interested in why we do what we do.

Most modifications have the goal of making the car appear longer, lower, and wider. Early customs were often the owner's sole means of transportation, and today's on-the-ground stance was not an option. In my never humble opinion, a custom car dropped too far detracts from the grace of design by disrupting the smooth total package look. It becomes the focal point and takes away from the design. Check out Stan Baker's great sectioned and chopped '40 Ford. The car is coach built, correct down to its 16-inch white walls. The car is so well designed and executed that many of the changes may go unnoticed at first.

You may think early custom builders weren't smart enough to give their creations the severe chops so popular today. You should take into account the poor roads or even the lack of roads encountered by the driver of a customized car that served as sole means of transportation back then. Remember, form follows function.

I was reminded of this by Gary Emory, son of a legendary body man Neil Emory, of Valley Custom shop fame. Gary told me a story about a Valley customer who liked the big trunk on his sectioned '40 Ford, because it could hold all of his prospecting gear for excursions into the foothills to pan for gold. The car had practical, as well as aesthetic value.

Anyone who thinks it easy to walk into a workshop and create something new and improved, year after year, will never understand what it takes to be a customizer. Customizers are artists working with line and texture, form and color. They attempt to create something as close as humanly possible to a masterpiece.

All this dedication and drive can be a strain on health and family life, and many famous and near famous customizers have paid dearly.

Recently the cost of building a top-notch custom, even a traditional one, has gone nuts. Reports of flathead-powered '49 Fords and Mercs costing $80,000 and more seem totally whacked, but consider this—in the not too distant past, many custom shops had to rely on insurance collision work to survive. The custom car work had to take a back seat. In most cases the money from custom work did not compare to collision repair. Consider that today, repairing a slightly indented scratch on the lower half of a door, with solid color/clear coat paint, below the trim only (an easy job) costs more than $600. What does that make a single shaved door handle worth? Is it 10 times as much work? You better believe it is! Can you charge 10 times as much? No way! You can't charge six grand to shave a door handle.

Currently I consider my time worth $50 an hour for labor and $25 dollars each hour for material/overhead charge. That's $75 times, say 1,000 hours to build that near perfect shoebox Ford, inside out, top to bottom. The high-priced custom starts to make sense.

The backlash to these high costs is the popularity of less-than-perfect rods and customs, home-built and on the cheap. Not just the beater "rat rods" that look like someone is trying a little too hard to rebel, but many clean cars home-built or not, painted or not. Cars that remind us all that this is supposed to be fun stuff.

Today's street rod and custom car guys seem to be at very opposed poles in their automotive efforts. In the bad old days, many of the hop-up guys had a customized fat-fendered coupe or sedan for the girl friend or wife and kids to enjoy. Some street customs had hopped-up engines, and the line between hot rod and custom often got blurry.

The visual point of the racer's "form follows function" mindset really influenced the custom crowd. The chopped top coupes and sedans (with stock engines) looked fast just sitting still. Lots of '33 to '36 customs were built. When Detroit iron got big in the 1940s and 1950s the Caddys, Mercs, and the like were too heavy to be popular race car fodder, but the old styling practices stayed popular. Racer tricks like shaving lumpy door handles, along with hood and trunk trim, and the ultimate wind cheating practice of chopping tops stuck with us.

The irony is that despite the look of the custom cars, in many cases they were hampered in acceleration and performance by the oppressive weight of bodywork done in the lead. The now common slang term "lead sled" was a fighting insult and the possibility exists that this explains the popularity of shades or sunglasses worn by the custom car crowd. It was probably to hide a black eye or two.

A few custom car owners went for the gold in the performance department. Washington State's Doug Rice built the beautiful chopped and channeled custom '39 Ford shown in this book. It appears today having been restored by current owner Don Richardson of Richardson Customs in Hoquiam, Washington. Rice used to race the custom at the Shelton, Washington, Airport Drags in the early 1950s (rolling start quarter-mile). In 1953, Rice took the car to Bonneville for the first time. The car, powered by a 296-inch Merc flathead, made several strong runs and made it into several magazines and a book or two. And all this was on his honeymoon.

A side trip to LA produced a black deuce roadster highboy. A tow bar behind the '39 enabled the newlyweds to share the coupe for the long trip home.

Things got interesting when Rice broke the crankshaft in the '39. Rice's bride had to fire up the '32 roadster, which was still attached to the tow bar behind the '39, and push the custom with Rice at the wheel all the way back to Hoquiam. Rice said people on the road, who thought the '39 was towing the roadster, would smile and wave. The '32 roadster was lost in the shuffle years later, but the '39 and the marriage, have both survived the test of time.

It has been said that in modern times the three most important things in custom car building are attitude, attitude, and attitude. A few custom car builders outfit their cars for the performance image, and such an owner is "Flathead Jack" Schafer. I should clarify something here—when I use the term "modern" I'm referring to cars built lately. I'm definitely not referring to Schafer. I once asked Schafer what he thought about my plans to use a Chevy part on my flathead, and my ears are still ringing. He was right of course, and I will continue to rely on Schafer for advice and his fine selection of parts. He really know his stuff when it comes to flatheads.

Schafer's 276-ci-powered, no-nonsense '49 Mercury has been chopped and filled, nosed and decked, and corners everywhere rounded by Bill Reasoner. It was then dropped just right all around by Greg Westbury to finish a traditional custom treatment. Now we switch gears and the hot rod menace look takes over. Louvers are punched in the hood,

Moon racing disc wheel covers and a coat of flat black make the perfect foundation for the Art Himsl "arrest me" flame job. Hard to believe, but sometimes Schafer must think he's not making enough of a statement so the hood comes off (this happens a lot) and then Schafer isn't just driving, he's struttin' his stuff. Many customs had stock engines for good reason. Highly modified flathead six- and eight-cylinder engines could run hot and start hard, and finding points and other parts on a road trip could be tough.

The practice of installing near-stock overhead V-8s in customs helped tremendously in the drivability department. The stock engines no doubt contributed to the coast-to-coast dispersal of many famous customs and spread the fad by exposing rural America to some very famous customs. Case in point, I can remember as a young lad in Tacoma, watching Jim Foran cruise Busche's Drive-in in his Barrio-built full-custom '50 Merc convertible. Check out the car as it appears here, having been totally restored to better than original by Bill Warden. An unusual feature on Warden's Merc is the use of stock chrome trim for lights, but nonfrenched Buick taillights are adapted and blended into the Merc's rear quarter panels. Very unusual.

Traditionally customized Fords, Chevys, and other low-priced cars were disguised with parts from more expensive cars. Packard grills, Caddy grills and hub caps, Buick fender skirts and taillights, Packard tails, and Caddy rear fender sections, complete with tail lights were all popular. The idea was to make your old cheap car look newer or more expensive, not a copy of an existing high priced car, but an effort to capture the flavor of the best, most prestigious cars of the day. It was generally accepted practice to use only newer parts on older cars—'39 Ford taillights on a '36 Ford for instance. The use of older parts on a newer model was and is seldom done. A rare but very successful example of early parts on a later car is Bill Ross' stunning candy emerald green '46 Ford with a '38 Zephyr front end adapted.

Ross' car has received many awards, including the Barris Award at the 50th annual Grand National Roadster show in 1999. The '46 Ford body has '50 Buick fenders that are protected by a '49 Plymouth station wagon rear bumper. The '38 Lincoln Zephyr front fenders surround a '39 Zephyr grill. The headlights are frenched '39 Ford units. It's art deco on wheels.

Early cars were personalized to suit the owner's taste by bolting on goodies from the local auto supply store. These cars loaded with chrome trinkets were called goodie-wagons (and worse). The Hirohata Merc and nearly all the traditional customs have made use of my least-favorite custom accessory, the spotlight. In largely rural America, a working spotlight was a very useful addition, and many used cars that served as raw material for customs came already equipped with one.

Customizers noticed the way the chrome teardrop shape distracted the eye and made the top look lower. Many early customs had only one. Later customs had a second light added to the passenger side for balance and gave some advantage in the spotlight wars at the drive-in. The advent of the fake or dummy spots allowed the look without the work of mounting real Appletons.

The earliest custom I recall using spotlights was a chopped '34 Ford three-window with rear fender skirts. The real and dummy spots have been popular on every make and model for more than 50 years—must be a record for longest running custom accessory.

By now I hope you understand the reason you may see a '48 Cadillac grille in a '41 Ford custom but never the other way around. But hey, what do you do when your car is already a top of the line model with all the prestige that goes with it?

Paul Harper in Roslyn, Washington, is a man who knew what to do when Barbara Johnson brought him her '49 Cadillac convertible. Harper chopped the top 2-1/2 inches, then sectioned the trunk to remove the hump and blend it in with the lower top lines. All excess trim pieces (rag catchers) that detracted from the Caddy's beautiful lines were removed. The headlights were frenched, and absolutely nothing was done to detract from the Caddy's original design. Byers Custom Paint in Auburn, Washington, displayed the same restraint with the perfect black-violet pearl paint job. Bob Jasper of Tacoma did the white leather interior; the interior, the white top, and wide whites on '53 Caddy wire wheels, just shout Deluxe!

High-priced cars of the 1930s and 1940s had long straight sixes, straight eights, V-12, or even V-16 engines.

Naturally a long hood was required and became a very prestigious and prominent feature. The practice of shortening hood side trim made the custom's hood appear longer. When '52 Ford headlight rings were added to stubby fenders, it greatly increased the perceived length, and the highly prized long hood look was the result. I took a clue from the Barris Brothers' treatment on the Bob Hirohata '51 Mercury; not only did they use the '52 Ford rings, but they spaced them out another couple of inches to further the long nose effect. I did the same and also dropped the lights 2 inches closer to mother earth and tapered the fenders to match on Denny Hall's '51 Merc. A tapered section cut from the front of the hood avoided the too-high-hood syndrome.

The optical illusions or tricks customizers use are not limited to Fords and Mercs. Chevy and Plymouth cars respond beautifully, as do most models from the 1940s. Not too long ago, my pal Larry Andrews wanted me to make a few changes to his '48 Plymouth coupe. All changes were based on a single constant theme, creating a 1990s custom honoring custom techniques of the past.

Expensive production cars of the past used welded panels and leaded seams; cheaper cars simply bolted panels in place using cloth and cord fender welting to stop squeaks and seal out water. The first order of business was to mold in the rear fenders, or "seal them" as it was referred to in the 1940s. This eliminated the low-priced look. Same deal on the front fender seams and the center hood seam after the chrome was removed. Hood side trim was drastically shortened, and the square hood corners were rounded to soften the look. The stock headlight rings were welded to the fenders, and the fenders were extended with sheet metal to blend smoothly with a minimum of filler. This process was called "plating" in the 1950s. The stubby little coupe appears much longer now, but it's all visual—not 1 inch was added to the car's length. Stock taillight lenses were moved down lower on the body and frenched. A third lens was frenched into the trunk for a third brake light, blended into a special eyebrow for the license plate light over a traditional sunbeam plate in the trunk lid. The final finishing touch was a set of "Briz" DeSoto type ripple bumpers. DeSoto was the upgrade from Plymouth, and the bumpers have a more deluxe appearance.

The car has a very traditional custom look that has been finished by a proud new owner, Randy Cole of Castle Rock, Washington. Cole added V-8 running gear and a rich wine color to finish the outside in great style.

The masters of customizing in the past had many fine tricks in their bag. They did not, in most cases, make changes for change's sake, but employed optical illusions with line and color to achieve the desired effect. Study the fine photos in this book and enjoy both the photography and the cars for what they are, true automotive art.

—*Dick Page*

I took this photograph of Dick Page in his shop sometime in the early 1990s. The car he is working on is Denny Hall's '51 Mercury, and as you can see from the photograph, a considerable amount of metal work has been done. Dick is a consummate craftsman, and we have had many conversations involving the aesthetics and the reason for some of these modifications that customizing really is. The car has been chopped with slanted B pillars, which match the angle of the rear fender ends. Dick has also sectioned the hood and extended and dropped the front headlights. The bumpers have been lowered to help give the appearance of lowness without sacrificing the ride. There are many more modifications that have been worked into the car; and yes, these are important, as the overall look is sometimes in the details.

I had a chance to visit with Terry Hegman at his shop in December 2000. While there, I photographed the '51 Mercury that he has been working on, for himself. The car is in bare metal, which gives the viewer a direct visual idea of the craftsmanship that Terry has applied to all of the major modifications. The proportioning of this Merc is incredible and it has all been very well thought out, so nothing seems out of place or just an exercise in adding some custom feature for the sake of it. Everything works in a visual sense, and everything that Terry did to the car was for a visual reason in improving the overall look. If you check the profile of the car, you will notice how well the top-chop works with the rest of the body. It has been cut 3 inches in the front and 4 inches in the rear, and he added the '50 Merc rear window. The pillars have the perfect slant with the B-pillars matching the flow of the rear fenders. The workmanship is outstanding, but as I mentioned earlier, if the proportions are off, the best work in the world can't make it right. Terry's treatments to the headlights, the grille and surround, the taillights, and both bumpers all work toward making a singular statement. It all works and proportions out together, right down to the wheelwell openings and fender skirts, all of which have been modified, as have all the sharp corners on the hood, deck lid, and doors. Check out the details on this car if you ever get the chance. It is perfect. Terry's metalworking skills and his visual aesthetic are as good as I've seen anywhere.

Stan Baker's '40 Ford convertible is a step back in time to the days of coachwork customizing. This car is subtle, and it was sitting in the back row of a Northwest car event in the middle of bright colors. It is black on black on black, which means the workmanship has to be good, especially with the amount of cutting that was done this body. Stan emphasizes that there was nothing used on the car that wasn't available in the 1940s. It is all Ford Motor Company parts. The drivetrain is as it came from the factory. The body is a little different as it has been chopped 2-1/2 inches and sectioned 2-1/2 inches. The work Stan did in sectioning the hood and trunk area is amazing, and very proportionally correct. These areas are difficult to work with, as they also involve the firewall, hood hinges, dash, and steering up front and the obvious line just above the fenders in the rear. The car is quite simply gorgeous, and very well done. The 16-inch wheels and tall, skinny, and wide whitewall tires look as if there could not have been any other choices. It is all classic coachwork in the true sense.

177 Customs

Don and Irene Richardson's '39 Ford coupe has an interesting history, and not one you would normally expect from a custom. Doug Rice originally built the '39 Ford custom in the early 1950s. It was on the cover of *Rod and Custom* magazine and featured in *Hot Rod* in 1954. Besides being driven daily and shown in the West, it was raced and timed at Bonneville in 1952, 1953, and 1954, as well as seeing some drag-strip time. Don and Irene now own the car, and it has been freshened and brought to the state you see in the photograph by Don. You see, Don and Irene's business is just that, building hot rods and customs out of Hoquiam, Washington. The body modifications are extensive, with the top being chopped 3.5 inches in the front and 4.5 inches in the rear. The body has been channeled 5 inches and sectioned 2.5 inches. The fenders were raised, with the rears also being widened by 2.5 inches. Also, '40 Ford doors and dash were added to the '39, as was a '42 Ford rear window. The hood was sectioned 5 inches to fit with the body sectioning. This is a major amount of cutting and reshaping on this body style. Keeping the proportions correct, and aesthetically pleasing, was a major undertaking, and the work that was done is beautiful. The oxblood and white interior was redone to match Gaylords original that was done in 1954. The car is now running a Chevy 350 with tripower, a turbo 350 transmission, and a '79 Impala 3:08 Posi-Traction rear end. Don repainted the '39 with Cabernet lacquer, and yes, the car gets driven.

Right
Bill and Linda Ross' emerald green '46 Ford custom threw me the first time I saw it. I wasn't sure what the original body was, as the modifications are extensive and well carried out. The quality of the work is evidenced in the multiple awards the car has taken, including the Barris Award at the 50th Annual Oakland Roadster Show. This is a home-built car with only the upholstery and the paint being farmed out. Bill is a craftsman with metal and hand-worked all of the modifications, which start in back with '50 Buick fenders, frenched glass lenses, and '49 Caddy skirts. The peaked deck lid flows into a license plate surround and a '49 Plymouth wagon bumper. The windshield opening was raised 2 inches and chopped 3 inches; it holds in place an original Hauser Carson top and a set of original 112 Appelton spots. The front clip is from a '38 Lincoln Zephyr with a '39 Zephyr grille and frenched 1939 Ford headlights. The convertible sits on a hand-built frame and a full adjustable airbag suspension system. The horsepower comes from an original '57 T-Bird 312-inch Y block "E" engine. The House of Colors candy emerald green paint gives the car the *Emerald Envy* moniker. I photographed this car twice, once in gray primer, and once when it was finished, at the Moscow, Idaho Airport, late in the evening.

179 Customs

Bob Casey's '47 Buick Roadmaster is one of America's most classically styled bodies. Bob picked up the car from his wife's father's place in Montana and spent four years doing what he called a low-dollar rebuild with a mild custom treatment. He swapped out the original straight-eight engine for a 401-ci Buick Nailhead V-8 and a turbo -400 from a $600 '66 Buick Electra, from which he also pulled the power brakes. Lowering blocks in the back and cut-coils in the front bring the long Buick down to a nice and more modern road height. The long hood had a fair amount of louvers punched in it, and other than shaving the rear deck and adding dual reflectors in the rear fenders, not much has been done to the car. The car is beautiful from any angle and looks perfect with the smooth chrome wheels, baby moons and wide white-wall tires. The black-cherry paint, and very tasteful pinstriping, all help toward the finished look. The original trim and stainless, with the exception of the deck lid pieces, have been left on the Buick. Finding a car with all that in place was a bonus.

"Flathead Jack" Schafer has the ultimate company car: this chopped, lowered, louvered, flamed, and, of course, flathead-powered, '49 Merc. This traditional, edgy, and absolutely cool custom looks equally good without the extensively louvered hood in place. That's when you see the very clean and crisp hot-rod 276-inch flathead that gets this time-warp Merc down the road. Driven without the hood actually showcases many of the parts that Jack sells though his business, so it gets driven that way often. Jack's Mercury spent seven months in Bill Reasoner's shop getting the top chopped as well as the many other fine custom touches that were done to it. The top was cut 5 inches in the front and 4.5 inches in the rear, with the rear window "laid down" rather that cut, which gives a little more visibility as well as blending in with the lines of the trunk. The basically stock suspension was reworked by Greg Westbury to take out 7.75 inches in front and 5.5 inches in the rear. The beautiful flames really hit you when viewed against the flat black paint. They were laid out and painted by Art Himsel. The rolled and pleated black Naugahyde interior, the wide whites, and traditional Moon discs are in keeping with the look that this Merc has—that it could have been built in the 1950s. I photographed Jack's Merc at sunset out in the Concord Pavilion parking lot.

Jerry Hanger's 1949 Cadillac Coupe de Ville was completed transformed into what you see in the photograph by Jerry and his friends at Jerry's shop, which is actually Jerry's Transmission Service. He said it was his first top chop and Kandy paint job. The car is stunning, especially in the sun. The natural lines of this Cadillac two-door hardtop, and the feel of overall length, are further enhanced by the 3-inch top chop and the lowness of the car. The hood, deck lid, and doors have been shaved of all trim, with the exception of the hood ornament and center spear. Jerry then decided to french the headlights and smooth the rear quarters by removing the side trim. The smooth chrome wheels and narrow whitewalls work with the lowered car perfectly, helping to set off the metallic silver-underbased Kandy tangerine paint job and the all-white interior.

Dennis and Carlene Moore's '49 Cadillac sedanette was finished in 1994. Al Gerard and his son, Al Jr., are responsible for all the metal work. Dennis said they exchanged design ideas many times before cutting into the two bodies they had to work with. The top was actually chopped 3-1/2 inches and slid back, with the front windshield being laid back rather than cut. The treatment of the lines going from the windshield to the front of the hood, which slopes down and was accomplished with pie-cuts, is perfect. With the top being moved back, it was necessary to shorten the trunk 3-1/2 inches and extend the rear quarter windows the same amount. Again, the line of the rear in conjunction with the top is exemplary and clean, and is augmented by the removal of the B-pillars. The rear fenders, keeping the beautiful original Cadillac fins, were welded on and blended to help with the lines. Smoothing the bumpers and adjusting their relationship with each respective end adds to the overall finished quality. The beautifully painted black contrasts nicely with the all-leather beige interior. The smooth and mellow sound coming through the 2-1/4 inch exhaust and Flowmaster mufflers, comes from a mildly reworked 512-ci Cadillac engine, with enough torque to move the Cadillac down the road in style.

Barbara Johnson is not new to the custom car world. In fact, when she found this '49 Cadillac convertible, she owned a chopped '51 Mercury coupe. Having always wanted a customized convertible, Barbara took the Cadillac to Paul Harper in Roslyn, Washington, for modifications. The transformation produced a rolling work of art. Paul chopped the original folding top 2-1/2 inches, then proceeded to drop the mechanism into the rear fender wells. Next came a sectioned deck lid and other body modifications to enhance the Caddy's original and beautiful design. You have to look closely for the modifications, as they are subtle. Byers Custom Paint Shop in Auburn, Washington, sprayed the black-violet-pearl paint, and Bob Jasper of Tacoma stitched the white leather interior. Mechanically, the stock engine was traded for a balanced '60 Caddy 390-ci V-8, which was improved by adding a three-deuce carburetor setup and a hotter cam. Handling the increased power is a durable turbo -400 automatic transmission. Coker wide-whitewall radials mounted to a set of beautiful '53 Cadillac wire wheels keep the custom rolling in style. The first year out of the shop, Barbara put 5,400 miles on the odometer, traveling to Paso Robles, California, and on to Davenport and Des Moines, Iowa.

Bill Worden had owned 13 '49–'51 Mercs before he found this one. He had also admired and always wanted an original Barris Custom, so when this Barris-built '50 Merc convertible became available in 1978, Bill stuck a deal and took it home. Sam and George Barris worked their magic on the car in 1951, for Ralph Testa in Hollywood, California. The cost for the work and construction was a grand total of $1,750. It stayed in Southern California for some time and was featured in many early magazines, including *Hop Up* and the very first *Rod & Custom* magazine. Subsequently, the car went through various owners, ending up in the Northwest, where Bill found the car. Larry Foss did the body and paint restoration, and Bob Jasper worked his magic on the interior and top. Bill has high compliments for both regarding their talents and professional work ethics. All of this restoration was to the period-perfect specs that Bill wanted, with the only concession to modern convenience being the added power steering. He has owned hard-turning Mercs before. The engine is a fully balanced and blueprinted 331-ci Cadillac with a four-speed hydro transferring the power to the stock rear end. The Merc has been lowered 5 inches in front and 7 inches in the rear. The Carson padded top had 4 inches taken out of the front, tapering back to a 6-inch chop in the rear. It has a classic profile. The grille is a floating Henry J unit, the headlights have been frenched, and all the seams have been molded. Side trim from a '47 Buick was added, and the taillights are from a '49 Buick, turned sideways. The exhaust exits through the rear bumper, as Barris originally fashioned it. The coral blue-purple paint was matched from original paint found on the gravel pan under the front bumper. All glass pieces are the originals cut by Sam and George Barris. A classic it is, and it looks beautiful cruising the highways, which it does.

Jim and Suzi Hale owned this '50 Mercury custom when I photographed the car in Puyallup, Washington, in 1995. The car has been chopped 3-3/4 inches in the front, 4-3/4 inches in the rear, and made into a hardtop. The headlight and taillights have been frenched, all seams have been filled, and all corners have been rounded. The '54 Chevy grille has 15 teeth and the stock front and rear bumpers use '51 Kaiser guards and bullets. The candy, brandywine-colored paint was sprayed by Dale Withers, who is a very well-known and highly regarded body and paint man in the Portland, Oregon, area. The Cadillac seat was cut down 5 inches for headroom clearance and upholstered by Jim Engers of Beaverton, Oregon, to match a car from a '56 *Car Craft* magazine. All the inside and outside stainless trim molding was reshaped to fit the hardtop. The Mercury has been subframed with a 1974 Chevy Nova, which explains the use of a big-block Chevy 454 and turbo -400 transmission.

Darrel Wark's '50 orange Mercury custom pulled up next to Dennis and Debbie Kyle's '32 Ford roadster when I was looking over their hot rod at the 1991 Bonneville Speedweek Event. They matched colorwise and looked right timewise. The 4-inch top-chopped Merc drove in from Kansas under full flathead power, which is Darrel's other passion. He calls the car The *Kansas Tornado*, and had Ed "Big Daddy" Roth add the moniker to the corner of the shaved deck lid.

Below

I photographed Jack Aiken's '50 Mercury convertible in front of a big canvas backdrop that another photographer had set up to photograph cars on. He allowed me to get this shot. I guess it didn't work out to be financially or logistically feasible to continue, as I didn't see him back the next year. It is expensive as hell to set this stuff up, and I know he wasn't charging nearly enough for what he was going through, but it was probably what the market would bear. I don't know much else about the car.

Right top

Paul Harper builds customs out of Roslyn, Washington. You remember the television series *Northern Exposure*. Well, that was where some of it was shot, which overrode the town for a couple of years and has absolutely nothing to do with Paul's '51 Mercury convertible. Paul builds and customizes cars in the 1950s tradition. There is quite a bit of work in the car beyond the normal dechroming and removing trim. The headlights and rear fender skirts

have been frenched, and all the door corners have been rounded. The rear fenders have been extended over the lower half of '54 Merc taillights, and he used a '49 Buick rear bumper. Paul added a 4-1/2 inch chopped Carson top to the equation with a '34 Ford roadster back window. The front end uses a '50 Merc grille shell and the front bumper has been filled. The drive train is Mercury, but the engine is a 1959 390-ci Cadillac with four Stromberg 97 carburetors on a Horne manifold. The body sits on a '50 Merc chassis and has been lowered with spindles in front and lowering blocks in the rear. The metallic raspberry paint on the exterior matches the raspberry and cream rolled and pleated interior.

Right bottom

I saw this bare-metal '50 Chevy business coupe at the Muroc Reunions in 1999 and knew I had to get some photographs of it. Fabian Valdez owns the car and did all the work on it, which involves some pretty extensive customizing. The fact that it was in bare metal intrigued me, especially out on the dry-lake bed in the desert light. What also intrigued me was the proportioning that had been so well thought out and executed with all the modifications. The car just looked right. The top has been chopped 3-1/2 inches in the front and 4 inches in the rear. The front end is being reworked for a '49 Cadillac grille, and the headlights were not finished. Fabian is running a Chrysler front bumper and to work with the 5-inch stretched rear quarters, he is using a Packard rear bumper. When we will see all of this finished, I'm not sure, for Fabian has been bitten by the Bonneville (salt fever) and dry-lakes racing bug and is already working on a race car. He was involved with the S.C.T.A. at Muroc in helping out with the event in 1999, and was driving at the 2000 event. I also ran into Fabian and Willow at Bonneville, as they had come in with the Norm Benham crew and were helping out Joaquin Arnett and the Bean Bandits.

187 Customs

Willow Kirk's '54 Chevy 210 is a straight forward, straight-six-powered, old 1950s style custom. The original drive train is intact, with the rear suspension C-notched to help the ride. The car has been lowered, in keeping with the overall 1950s look. The top has been chopped 5 inches, it has been nosed and decked (emblems removed), and the headlights have been frenched. Fabian Valdez reworked the taillights into ones similar to the *Moonglow* Chevy custom of earlier times. Fabian also sprayed the custom semigloss paint. You will have to excuse the dust, as I photographed Willow's custom after it had spent a couple of days out on the dry-lake dirt at the Muroc Reunion in 2000—there is a "reality" patina to the car. Willow purchased the Chevy as an original, from the original owner.

Below left
Mike O'Brien's first statement about the '55 Buick Special custom is that it taught him the true meaning of patience. Actually, this is Mike's second '55 Buick Special. The first one he owned when he graduated from high school in 1966. He said they were cheaper than Chevys, as they were not popular among the teenagers of the time, and ecologically he was saving a stylish and comfortable car from the crusher. I have never figured out why more of these cars were not as collectable as others. At various times during the 1940s and 1950s, Buick, Cadillac, Oldsmobile, and Pontiac had some beautiful cars, as did Chrysler in the mid-1950s. They were very nice rides, and I expect the customizers will now start using them on a larger scale. They are still out there and they are, or just were, affordable. John Bulato of John's Street Rods did all of the frame and engine work, and the Buick rests on a '68 Chevy Nova chassis and suspension. The bodywork and custom modifications were handled by Joe and Dave at Dragon Custom in the Whittier area. The headlights have been frenched, the hood and door corners have been rounded, and the car has been shaved and decked. The classic Packard taillights were worked into the rear fenders, and the dark purple and violet paint colors were applied by Rudy at the Parkside Motors shop in Montebello, California. Steve, at Absolute Custom Painting in Orange, did the ghost flames. The Buick was photographed at Paso Robles, California, in 2000, just after sunset.

When I first saw Larry Foss' '53–'56 Ford F-100 pickup, two things visually hit me. The Prestige wheels were at that time new and unusual, and the dual landing lights were frenched into the lower raised and rolled front pan. The more I looked at it, the more I realized what had been done to it. The top had been chopped 3 inches, with the rear window left the full size. The front fenders were sectioned 1-1/4 inches to eliminate the front parking lights and to match up with the raised front pan. The rear fenders were widened 3 inches and the rear pan was hand-rolled into a double-chin style to eliminate that inverted breadbox look prevalent with aftermarket pans. The original Ford frame was mated with a Buick front clip, hence the Buick 455 engine, turbo -400 transmission, and power steering. What started off as a "Foss Bros. Rod & Custom" shop truck is now a very comfortable ride that is too nice to haul parts. Maybe next time.

One of the reasons I was attracted to Brenda and Dave Kreg's '56 Oldsmobile Holiday 88, was that I had a red and white '55 Olds convertible when I was in high school. They are great cars. Brenda and Dave's Olds is a mild 1950s-style custom. It's been nosed, decked, shaved, and louvered and it rides on chrome-reversed wheels with 3-inch-wide whitewall tires. Air Ride Technologies allows the car to sit right on the ground, and still be at a legal driving height when moving. The three-stage, Sikkins laser red and pearl white colors of paint were applied by Patrick Skahan at Patrick Enterprises. The white rolled and pleated interior is matched by the white rolled and pleated fender wells. The drive train is all Oldsmobile, but it's a 455 and turbo -400 hooked up to the stock rear end.

Art Wohlsein did what I hope to see more of in the near future within the custom-car culture. He took a good, solid 1950s car, in the form of a '56 Chrysler Windsor two-door hardtop, and created a mild custom that is different, just because he chose a car that not everybody is working with. He is ahead of the curve on this. I expect to see more of this type of custom in the next few years, in part because it is a reachable ride financially. Art nosed, decked, and shaved the car before painting it with this beautiful green and white sunburst primer. He also added some '60 Rambler bumperettes in the rear. The interior is traditional tuck and roll. The A-arms were dropped and the coils were cut to get the proper ride height. All the custom work on the car, and the makeover, was performed by Starlight Speed & Kustom, in Vancouver, Washington, with just a little help from his friends, Brent Housley and Kevin McCarthy, on the paint.

Mark Morton picked up a '65 Buick Riviera with a dual four-barrel carbureted 401-ci engine. He then removed the door handles, badges, moldings, and the front plate, had it painted BMW glacier green by Lou at Dreamers in Downey, and then had it lowered by having ADF in Whittier install an air-ride setup. He added some 1-1/8-inch whitewalls on 15x7-inch Buick Skylark wire wheels, and called it good. I like it. It is the way we used to do it in earlier times. No heavy body modifications, but the right car with the right things done to it, and it rides very, very low.

INDEX